365

DAYS OF PRAISE

Deacon Steve Greco

ISBN-13: 9781495317675

ISBN-10: 1495317676

Acknowledgement

I thank God for His guidance, support, encouragement and most of all, His love. I wish to thank my wife Mary Anne, who has inspired me to have a personal relationship with Christ. I am grateful for my son Mark, who encouraged me and used his time and talent to help develop this book; Katie Hughes who worked countless hours in helping me write questions and providing me with great insight; and Ronnie Martin for her outstanding editing!

Introduction

By Tillman Nechtman, PH.D.

In his first letter to the Thessalonians, St. Paul admonishes us to "pray without ceasing."[1]

What exactly does that mean? Pray without ceasing? I have things to do. The kids need to get to school. Somebody has to cook dinner. There is always dirty laundry to be washed. There is life. I'm busy. How in the world can I do all that I need to do if I am ceaselessly praying? Surely, St. Paul's commandment is better suited to those living monastic lives than it is to me! Right?

Perhaps not.

Many years ago, I read about an interview Mother Teresa of Calcutta had given I cannot recall now what I was reading way back then or even the context of the interview, but I do remember that the interviewer did, rather incredulously, ask

[1] 1 Thessalonians 5:17

Mother Teresa how she got anything done in a given day if she indeed prayed a full rosary every morning as she claimed to do. Mother Teresa's answer was sublime. "How would I get anything done if I did not pray my rosary?"

In that simple, disarming question, Mother Teresa turned the tables on our increasingly cynical and deeply secular modern world, for she highlighted an aspect of her own faith that is as profoundly countercultural as it is (and I say this sadly) uncommon.

Mother Teresa had a deep faith in the truth that she could do nothing without the power of prayer and spiritual reflection in her life. True, were she to skip her morning rosary, she might have added actual minutes to her working day, but would they have been efficacious minutes? Would the work she accomplished in them or in any of the other minutes of her waking life have been as grace-filled and powerful as they were as the result of her rosary prayer?

If we look to the life and witness of Blessed Teresa of Calcutta, the answer is surely no.

Prayer, spiritual reflection, and religious contemplation are as nourishing to us as is the food we eat at meals. It is, so the Christian tradition assures us, restorative, energizing and empowering. It is essential, which is perhaps why the Christian tradition has such a rich history of daily spiritual reflection. Whether we consider the Liturgy of the Hours (also known as the Daily Office), the ancient devotional practice of the Angelus, the contemplative practice of reading holy Scripture known as lectio divina, the Ignatian self-examining, or the previously mentioned exercise of praying the rosary, Christianity is richly supplied with prayerful routines that could help us pray without ceasing.

Still, though, that question burns in my mind. How do I accomplish all I need to do in a day if I pause so often to pray the rosary, read the Daily Office, contemplate holy Scripture, engage in a self-examine (much less the two examinations a day recommended by St. Ignatius of Loyola), or recite the Angelus?

In the book that you now hold in your hands, Deacon Steve Greco offers us two answers to that question.

First, Deacon Steve offers us a new volume in what has become a very rich, contemporary genre – the daily devotional book. Daily devotional books are founded on the notion that Christians do well to take even as little as six minutes out of every day to reflect on aspects of their faith. Recent studies have revealed the shocking fact that the majority of American Catholics do not even read one spiritual, religious, or theological book in any given year. Devotional books like this one allow us to digest a book slowly, at a safe pace, in small daily doses.

They allow us, in short, to integrate spiritual reading into our daily life without the kind of commitments we might fear from more time-intensive activities like the Daily Office or, even, a full rosary.

Devotional books have, as I noted above, proliferated in the past few decades. Volumes highlight daily readings from the Popes – including, but not limited to, books from Pope John Paul II and Benedict XVI. There are volumes by lay apologists like G.K. Chesterton and C.S. Lewis. I've seen a volume exclusively featuring the thoughts of converts to Catholicism and others featuring a daily saint or masterpieces of Catholic iconography and art. Some of these books have even featured great Catholic thinkers from the past whose voices and names might otherwise be less familiar to us today. Archbishop Fulton Sheen, the long-time host of the Emmy-winning Catholic televangelical program "Life is Worth Living," Monsignor Ronald A. Knox, Cardinal John Henry Newman and Arnold Lunn might all be grouped in this category, though it is a sad fact that such notables as Evelyn Waugh, the Catholic convert and author of *Brideshead Revisited*, are also largely lost to us as spiritual writers except in some of these daily compilations of spiritual reflections.

While adding richly to the tradition of daily devotional books, though, Deacon Steve's reflections stand apart from the crowd, and, in doing so, they offer us a second way of answering that nagging question – how do I get life done while also praying without ceasing. For, what you will find as you read Deacon Steve's daily meditations on faith, Scripture, and life is that there is no separation between the category of "daily life" and the life of faith for Deacon Steve. Here, rather, we find a successful businessman, a devoted husband, a loving father, and an ordained Catholic leader for whom faith is the thread that stiches the pieces of his life into one fabric. Here we find a husband for whom his wedding anniversary is cause to reflect on the Biblical origins of the marital institution, a father for whom his children's birthdays are causes and opportunities to reflect on the inheritance God grants to those who truly believe, a business man who turns to faith to release the anxieties wrought by a topsy-turvy economy. A man, in short, for whom faith is the foundation upon which all else rests.

In reading these meditations, I am reminded of an anecdote that Archbishop Fulton Sheen once told. In Sheen's story, a lawyer was told that he was terminally ill. His business partner, a Catholic, approached his long-time associate, advising that if he was indeed about to die he ought best to make his peace with God. Having never heard his partner speak of his faith previously, the dying attorney asked, "If Christ in your Church has meant so little to you during your life that you never once spoke to me, how can it mean anything to me at my death."[1]

Sheen's point—and, I might add, Deacon Steve's example—is that for those of us who truly believe, our faith, our love of Christ, our passion for our own salvation ought to manifest itself in all that we do. Sheen was quite clear on this point. "Every single action in your daily work," he wrote, "whether sweeping the street or teaching classes, can be made a prayer. Every action is a kind of blank check that has value only if the name of our Lord is signed to it. That is why St. Paul said, "Whether you eat or drink, or whatever you do, do it in the name of Christ."[2] Sheen had a great couple of words to describe this manner of living, this manner of doing, this manner of being in the world. If actions were done with divine intention they were "divinized and sacramentalized."[3]

Sacramentalized. Imagine that! Every action you do—as a parent, as a lawyer, husband or wife, a community volunteer, everything—becomes a sacrament so long as you do it with prayerfulness. Isn't that awesome?

---

[1] Archbishop Fulton Sheen, Your Life is Worth Living: The Christian Philosophy of Life (Schnecksville, PA: St. Andrew's Press, 2001), 195.

[2] Ibid. 346.

[3] Ibid.

Awesome, yes. Easy? No. As we read in the pages of this book, there are times we stumble, times we falter. But, the key is to keep trying. Take up the call, give six minutes back to God. Read a bit of Scripture, take in the words of a spiritual guide, meditate, reflect and pray on the text and the guidance. See how it absorbs into your life. Soon, you may find that the very actions you did yesterday have new meaning as you do them today precisely because you do them as prayerful actions. Precisely because you do them, to quote the motto of the Jesuit order "Ad maiorem Dei gloriam" ("for the greater glory of God"). The same things you did yesterday, you now do as sacraments; if all we do, we do as sacraments, then is it not true that every breath we take is a prayer? And, if that is true, then is it not equally true that, by living in God, we pray without ceasing? Why, yes, I think it is. And so, we come full circle. We find that not only can we pray constantly and still live, but also that by living properly, we pray perpetually. We find, in short, that we can live our lives even as we live them the way God intended for us to do – as a people with heaven inside of us.

January 1

2 Corinthians 5:17 "So whoever is in Christ is a new creation: the old things have passed away; behold new things have come."

How exciting! A new day, in a New Year! Full of hope and promise. Jesus is calling us to a new wineskin, a new approach to our life. For once, we pray that God truly takes over our life. Not just talk, but in reality. Not just when we feel like it, but through faith, we sincerely ask God's will to become our will. This is the only way we can develop into a new creation.

How do we do it? It sounds great, but what happens when life gets tough and we have to get results? Can I trust God to pay the bills? I only know that the old way doesn't work. The new way is Christ's way.

Jesus, I pray that you live in me each day of this year. Be with me in a way that I will always know your comfort, peace and joy.

What can you change to make your life more Christ-centered? What are some ways you can trust and put your life in God's hands?

January 2

Matthew 5:14-16. "You are the light of the world. A city set on a mountain cannot be hidden. Nor do they light a lamp and then put it under a bushel basket; it is set on a lampstand, where it gives light to all in the house. Just, so your light must shine before others, that they may see your good deeds and glorify your heavenly Father."

Speed ahead 100 years; you are now with the Lord in heaven. What legacy did you leave behind? For what are you remembered? How much money you made? Does anyone care about the titles you had? Or do the fruits of your life depend on the light in your life? The light that goes forth to spread God's Word and love for all to see and hear? How do we illuminate our jobs and activities so that they become the light of Christ in the world?

I pray that today and this year we may be bold enough to be the light of Christ for all

What are the things you can do that will show you are the light of Christ?

January 3

Acts 4:31. "As they prayed, the place where they were gathered shook and they were all filled with the Holy Spirit and continued to speak the word of God with boldness."

My wife Mary Anne and I start each day in prayer and Scripture. How else can God communicate what we are to do that day? The many decisions of the day will not be made in vain or alone. God will guide and lead us.

In prayer with my wife and prayer partners, this Scripture kept coming up as very important for the release of the Holy Spirit in our lives and for the power of the Lord to manifest in us.

Today, Lord, I ask for Your miracles in my ordinary times. May I speak your words with boldness. May I speak of love and show Your gentleness. I praise You for being the God of love!

Do you lack the courage to be bold while speaking of the Scriptures? Do you speak of the love God the Father has for His people? Look to the Scriptures!

John 15:5 "I am the vine, you are the branches. Whoever remains in me and I in him will bear much fruit, because without me you can do nothing."

God wants to use you in a mighty way this coming year. How do you know what God wants for you? Pray! Pray! Pray!

The most important thing is being in the presence of God and being open to His Love. In this way, you bear fruit that builds His kingdom. Without your focus on God, nothing you do matters. It is the only way to be successful in God's eyes. Associate with people who remind you of this reality. Be confident! God has something wonderful for you this year!

Lord; help us be the branches connected to the vine of Your love. Help us to decrease as You increase within us. We praise You for allowing us to produce fruit for Your vine!

How can you change to be less of yourself and more of God? How can your life bear fruit for the Lord?

January 5

Isaiah 41:10 "Fear not, I am with you;/ be not dismayed; I am your God./ I will strengthen you, and help you,/ and uphold you with my victorious right hand of justice."

Starting anything new—a life goal, personal project, business, job, etc.—can be frightening. Yet, Jesus is forever by our side, whispering, "Fear not for I am with you always." The great test for us is to walk by faith and not allow fear to enter our lives. When we do that, we receive the peace of Christ, now and forever!

The reality in my life is that I truly know, in the depth of my soul, that God is my light, my salvation and my shelter. When I trust in him, I have no fear.

Lord, give me the strength to get through the darkest moments of the day. Let Your light shine in the darkness of my faltering faith. I praise You for the gift of faith!

Ask the Lord to increase your faith! How does being in the presence of God give you strength in difficult times?

Joshua 1:9 "I command you: be firm and steadfast! Do not fear nor be dismayed, for the LORD, your God, is with you wherever you go."

Anyone who has ever been in sales or traveling for business knows that life is far from glamorous. Hotel rooms feel like prisons, and airports remind us of people being herded to destinations unknown. One can look around and see individuals who stare blankly and seem sad, lonely and confused.

However, the joy of the Lord and the Holy Spirit can remain with us always, even away from home. We are led to encounter God's children and those who Jesus wants us to love and evangelize. That makes the trip much more exciting and worthwhile!

Lord, let me see Your presence in faraway places and destinations. I praise You for being my constant companion wherever I go.

Do you look to the Lord when you need comfort or feel lonely? How do you connect with the joy of the Lord in times of loneliness and sadness?

January 7

Acts 18:9-10 "Do not be afraid. Go on speaking, and do not be silent, for I am with you. No one will attack and harm you for I have many people in this city."

Jesus is a God of hope and encouragement. He tells us that we are never alone. God's people are everywhere. They will open doors for you. They will guide you and give you gentle correction.

The enemy tries to confuse and cause doubt. It is important to recognize that when we speak, it is the Holy Spirit speaking through us. Yes, God begins to take over our lives, our jobs, our every moment of the day.

Lord, may You connect me with Your people wherever I am. Let me receive Your light through them. Let me feel Your love and Your encouragement. May I be bold in loving all people I meet today. I praise You for the gift of boldness and the gift of evangelism.

How do you evangelize? Words? Actions? Prayers?

Deuteronomy 7:12-15 "As your reward for heeding these decrees and observing them carefully, the LORD, your God, will keep with you the merciful covenant which he promised on oath to your fathers. He will love and bless and multiply you; he will bless the fruit of your womb and the produce of your soil...You will be blessed above all peoples. ..."

God's promises are real, not to be ignored or taken lightly. If we let Him lead us and take over our lives, we will be blessed. This blessing is a supernatural gift from God for His children, whom he loves beyond what we can ever comprehend.

When you walk with the Lord, everything around you is blessed, including your spouse, children, family, house, job, friends and ministries.

Lord, allow me to receive your blessings today. Open my heart to hear Your voice. Help me to follow Your decrees. I praise You for being the gift of eternal grace!

How do you show an open heart to the Lord? Do you pray and focus on His love to receive His gift of eternal grace?

January 9

John 15:16-17 "It was not you who chose me but I who chose you and appointed you to go and bear fruit that will remain, so that whatever you ask the Father in my name he may give you. This I command you: love one another."

In life, most of us want to believe we are in control of most everything that happens to us. If we think we are not in control, then anxiety quickly sets in.

When we realize that without God we can do nothing, and that He has chosen us, everything changes. We have a new leader, and it is not someone from this world. It is our eternal Father who is gentle, loving and less concerned about our successes and more interested in our faith and obedience.

Lord, let me realize today that the only true and lasting fruit that I will bear comes from You. Let me reflect Your love with others today and every day. I praise You for the gift of true life!

Do you feel like God has chosen You to serve Him? How are you currently bearing fruit in your life?

January 10

John 16:23-24 "...whatever you ask the Father in my name he will give you. Until now you have not asked anything in my name; ask and you will receive, so that your joy may be complete."

This promise definitely seems too good to be true. If I ask for success in life this year will I receive it? What if I throw in a new car? What does it mean to ask in "His" name. If I ask in His name, I am asking as His ambassador...in "His" will as "His" surrogate.

Jesus always receives what He asks because He prays in the will of the Father. When we pray in the will of Jesus, it will be to build up his kingdom and to love and bless His people.

Lord, let me manifest Your will today in all things. Allow me the grace to ask anything as Your servant, so that Your kingdom will be built in all that I do. I praise You for the gift of the Holy Spirit!

How can you use your gifts of the Holy Spirit to better serve God and His people.

January 11

Matthew 7:18 "A good tree cannot bear bad fruit, nor can a rotten tree bear good fruit."

To be one with Christ is the goal, beginning with the realization that our life's goals only bear fruit if God is at the center of them. When we surrender ourselves, God takes over—molding, shaping and guiding us. He does this because He has already chosen us before the dawn of time to be His. Rejoice and bear eternal fruit for our Lord! He truly wants us to bloom where we are planted and to bear fruit that is everlasting peace.

Today, Lord, help me see Your hand in every aspect of the day, whether big or small. I praise You for being my spiritual eyes today!

How do you praise God for the blessings He has bestowed upon you? Are your eyes open to receive His gifts?

January 12

Ruth 1:16 "…'Do not ask me to abandon or forsake you! For wherever you go, I will go, wherever you lodge, I will lodge, your people shall by my people, and your God my God.'"

Today is my wife's birthday. I have never known a holier or more blessed person. We have been blessed to be married more than 45 years.

When we made the decision a number of years ago to be bicoastal, she wanted a dog to bring to New Jersey and return some day with us to California. Wherever Mary Anne went, she wanted the dog to be with her. You guessed it! We named the dog Ruth because of the today's verse. For wherever my wife went, Ruth was with her, blessing her with her comfort and presence.

Lord, thank You their presence with me in person or in spirit, wherever I go. I praise You for the gift of family.

How do you show your family your love and appreciation? What is God calling you to do to better appreciate your family?

Exodus 14:13-14 "...'Fear not! Stand your ground and you will see the victory the LORD will win for today.... The LORD himself will fight for you; you only have to keep still.'"

Wow! God will fight for me? I only have to stand my ground and not run and hide as I often want to do? It seems too good to be true.

I am used to believing it is my talent and works that make the difference in my successes. It is obvious that God's way is not my way.

When I focus on Him, I don't need to worry about success in this world, because He will give me graces for today, tomorrow and all eternity.

Lord, I repent of my pride in thinking that I am the reason for my success. Help me to believe in You.

How in your life do you surrender to God's will? When do you decide to take over and tell God, "I can handle this?"

January 14

Joshua 3:13 "When the soles of the feet of the priests carrying the ark of the LORD, the Lord of the whole earth, touch the water of the Jordan, it will cease to flow...."

Nothing happens until we decide to play our role in God's equation. Our will must reflect God's will by our actions. The Israelites would have never been successful unless they "took action" by deciding to cross the Jordan.

What is your Jordan? What bold action do you need to take? Do it today! It is only then God's miracles will manifest.

Lord, help me today to have the courage to take action in the most difficult parts of my day and life, so that Your miracles may flow through me. I praise You for being the gift of all miracles in my life.

Do you live your life with courage? Do you recognize the big and the small miracles that God blesses you with?

Matthew 9:37. "…'The harvest is abundant but the laborers are few….'"

How do we make our life choices? Are we searching for fame, money, power or success? Do we choose out of fear? The goal should be the same for you and for me—to build God's kingdom. When this becomes reality, our plan becomes God's plan.

The measure of success is the degree of the Holy Spirit working through us.

In my experience, when we ask to be used by God, it happens every time. One-hundred percent! No doubt about it! Jesus will bring you people to love, to minister to and care for. Remember, ask and you shall receive!

Jesus, help me today to build Your kingdom—to help others see Your love.

Do you listen to Jesus when He is trying to tell you how you can help build His kingdom? How productive are you in building the Body of Christ?

Matthew 13:3-8 "A sower went out to sow, and as he sowed some seed fell on the path and birds came and ate it up. Some fell on rocky ground, where it had little soil. It sprang up at once because the soil was not deep, and when the sun rose, it was scorched and withered for lack of roots. Some seed fell among thorns, and the thorns grew and choked it. But some seed fell on rich soil and produced fruit of a hundred or sixty or thirty fold."

I believe we all are living the parable of the seed. All of us receive the message of salvation from the Lord. It is written on our hearts. If we allow the devil to reject this message, then we block the grace and blessings of Our Lord. However, for most of us, even if we do receive this grace, we allow the glamour of the world, the desire for wealth, pride and/or life's trials to choke out the abundant fruits of the Holy Spirit.

Lord, I pray that the seeds of our life will take root on fertile ground, so that we may build your kingdom.

How do you spread God's Word? Do you share your faith?

John 14:14 "If you ask anything of me in my name, I will do it."

What does it mean to ask in His name? It means that, through the power of the Holy Spirit, Jesus takes over our lives, and we take on His identity. It is Jesus within us praying to the Father through the Holy Spirit.

If you have children, you want them to ask you for your help. You want to give them grace and joy. How much more does our heavenly Father want to give us His spiritual blessings and gifts?

Lord, help me today to die to myself and receive Your presence in my life. Give me the grace to ask in Your will. I praise You for the power of the Holy Spirit connecting me with the love of Jesus.

Are you acting as a child of God? Do you ask for His guidance to fulfill the Word of God? Do you ask for His blessings, His grace, His everlasting love?

January 18

2 Corinthians 10:4-5 "[F]or the weapons of our battle are not of flesh but are enormously powerful, capable of destroying fortresses. We destroy arguments and every pretension raising itself against the knowledge of God, and take every thought captive in obedience to Christ."

It is critical that we know whom we are fighting! It is not the people who oppose us, but our spiritual enemies. The devil seeks to destroy any person, organization, ministry or family building God's kingdom.

The best way to defeat the enemy is to take captive every thought that is inconsistent with the will of Jesus. That means rooting out any sinful lust, gossip, dissension or discouragement. Anything in our lives that takes us away from the love of Jesus. Another critical way to defeat the enemy is to love others in Jesus name.

Lord, take over all thoughts I have today and purify them as a sacred aroma of Your love.

Do your thoughts get in the way of God's love for you? Ask Him to purify your soul?

Colossians 3:2 "Think of what is above, not of what is on earth."

With the many challenges of life, work and family, it is extremely difficult consider things beyond the present day. Everyday life frequently feels overwhelming to us, especially at the beginning of a new year.

What does it mean to think of things from above? It means to measure everything we are doing by spiritual realities. To focus on heavenly treasure and not earthly treasure. What are our priorities? Our focus? What do we think about?

Let us always put today's challenges in second place to the priority of serving God.

Lord, help me to focus on treasures from above and trust in You for treasures on earth. I praise You Lord for changing my heart.

Are you focusing on God's gift of everlasting life in heaven? Are you putting God first, developing a personal relationship with Him so that you can attain the treasures of heaven?

Romans 8:28 "We know that all things work for good for those who love God, who are called according to his purpose."

I suggest everyone who seeks God memorize this verse! How many times in our lives or careers do things fail to work out? I have often said, "Show me anyone who is successful, and I will show you someone who has overcome adversity." So, how does God overcome failure? Faith! It is by faith that everything will be used for His glory when we put it on the cross of redemption. Resurrection always follows!

A very spiritual teacher once said that when we die, our lives will flash before us. God will ask us if we want to change anything. If we are with the Lord, our answer will be "No." Why? Because we will see that God used everything for His good, and to change any of it would be to change the grace we have received from the Lord.

Lord, help me to rejoice through adversity, because through faith, resurrection is born.

Do you believe God turns all things to good? Rejoice!

January 21

Psalm 145:8 "The Lord is gracious and merciful, slow to anger and abound in love."

We often assess God in the same way as we consider our relationship with our earthly father. If our father was stern and difficult, we picture God as unforgiving, holding on to our sins and punitive.

If we had a loving and forgiving relationship with our father, then we can more readily accept this verse in Psalms.

The reality is that God is love. As love, He does not hold grudges, is always loving and welcoming, is merciful.

Heavenly Father, thank you for filling my heart with Your love. I praise You for giving me a holy earthly father and ask that You always watch over him.

When you go to the Father with your sins and ask for forgiveness, do you understand that His love is so great and that He has already forgiven you? He is the Father who understands our weakness better than we do and is already waiting for you to return to him. Be ready to forgive yourself when you go to Him!

Revelation 3:11 "I am coming quickly. Hold fast to what you have, so that no one may take your crown."

It is always fascinating to me that most of us live as if we are going to live forever. We try to build our kingdom, our empire and our wealth. Long after we need not worry about these things, we continue to be driven by them.

Scripture tells us we are a vapor that appears briefly and disappears. Life is all too short. We need to treasure each day as if it is our last, and use it to build God's kingdom.

The reward for us in heaven is the crown of life. Let's remember that this is what we are working toward.

Lord, I praise You and worship you always for the gift of wisdom. May I always ask for this great gift to serve your people.

Do you live life to the fullest with those around you by using the wisdom God has given you? Do you share the gifts, talents and wealth of this world with others? Our Lord provides these gifts and wants us to share them with all His children.

Colossians 3:12 "Put on then, as God's chosen ones, holy and beloved, heartfelt compassion, kindness, humility, gentleness, and patience."

To live the life of Christ, our behavior must be dramatically different from the world's. It may be tempting to respond in kind when hurt or slandered, but God's way is different. We are to be compassionate—to have the heart of Christ.

Today is my son Paul's birthday. I am blessed that he has the gifts of compassion, kindness, humility, gentleness and patience.

I praise God for him!

Lord, help me to reflect your compassion, kindness, humility, gentleness and patience with my family, friends, co-workers, and all the people I meet today. I praise You for giving me the gifts of the Holy Spirit.

Do you draw from your gifts of the Holy Spirit to become more Christ-like in your actions? Do you realize the best way to praise God is to use the gifts He has given you?

John 14:27 "Peace I leave with you; my peace I give to you. Not as the world gives do I give it to you. Do not let your hearts be troubled or afraid."

A comforting truth is contained in these words! True peace can only come from Jesus. Without it, our hearts are restless in search of Him. Jesus wants to take away all anxiety from our lives. When we say yes to His love, faith and joy, His peace takes over our lives.

Do not believe the lies of the enemy that would defeat God's peace. Know that God is holding you, gently, in the palm of His hand.

Lord, I desire only You today. Fill me with the grace of Your peace and dismiss all fear and anxiety. I praise You for the gift of peace!

How do you show God that you only desire Him? Do you truly believe that God is all you need in your life? How must you change to show your love for Him?

January 25

2 Corinthians 3:18 "All of us, gazing with unveiled face on the glory of the Lord, are being transformed into the same image from glory to glory, as from the Lord who is the Spirit."

This is one of my favorite Scripture passages because it depicts what happens when we surrender our life to Christ. When we are lost in sin and unbelief, we cannot see the Lord and how He is working in our life. We focus on this world and don't see God's grace.

Suddenly, we turn to God and we see everything dramatically differently. We focus on His love and grace. We rejoice in Him and what He is doing in our lives. Praise God now and forever!

Lord thank you for transforming me into your image. I praise Your name for using me to build your kingdom, in Jesus name, amen.

Though your troubles are difficult, do you praise God for His infinite wisdom and plan? Do you turn to Him in your difficult times so can He will guide you? You are not meant to journey this life without Him.

Romans 8:14 "For those who are led by the Spirit of God are children of God."

Are we aware that we are children of the most high God? That we can say "Abba," Father, because of what Jesus did on the cross and His resurrection?

If we truly focus on the reality that we are children of God, our anxiety begins to lessen. We know that all things work for good; that we are cared for and nourished. We need not fear, but rejoice and be glad!

Father, I praise Your name for choosing me to be Your child. I cry out to You Abba, Father!

Do you see our Father as loving and compassionate? Do you know how much He loves you? He sacrificed His only begotten Son for you! Do you trust Him in His ways and how He is working in your life? Your life will be joyful when you do!

Psalm 119:10 "With all my heart I seek you; do not let me stray from your commands."

We are told by psychologists that we make thousands of decisions each day. Some of these decisions bring us closer to God, and some take us away from Him. When we seek God first, we are filled with His Holy Spirit, and His spirit helps us make the right decisions.

God is always testing our hearts. What are our priorities? What is important to us? What do we truly seek in respect to our happiness? God will give us the desires of our heart. When we seek Him first, we will live a holy life and keep His commandments.

Father, thank you for helping me put You first in everything I do today, in Jesus name, amen.

How much do you love the Lord? Is He the center of your life? Do you believe in following His ways and loving His Son Jesus Christ?

January 28

Psalm 121:7-8 "The LORD will guard you from all evil;/ he will guard your life./ The LORD will guard your coming and going,/ both now and forever."

How would you like to be surrounded by God's protection? I believe His angels surround us and are at our side. Jesus asks us to trust Him—to be wrapped in His mantle and protected by His precious blood.

We are blessed to be children of God. Do we not protect our own children? How much more does God protect us from evil and harm!

Lord, I thank and praise You for protecting my family, friends and me.

How thankful are you for His eternal love and protection? When have you recognized His protection? Do you truly believe He protects you and your loved ones?

Psalm 120:1-2 "In my distress, I called to the LORD,/ and he answered me./ O LORD, deliver me from lying lip,/ from treacherous tongue."

There are days when I feel someone might be out to harm me by whispering untruths and gossiping about me or wishing me ill. I know God wants me to love and pray for them, and He will protect me from those treacherous tongues.

When we have a personal relationship with God, we can talk to Him intimately. We are not afraid to tell Him we need His help and protection. He will deliver us because He loves us!

Lord, protect me from those who seek to do me harm, and, Lord, prevent me from harming others. I praise You for Your protection.

Controlling your impulses can be quite difficult at times. What can you change to help curb your sinful behavior?

Romans 12:21 "Do not be conquered by evil but conquer evil with good."

There is evil in the world. No surprise there. People often stop at nothing to be successful or to make themselves feel important. The way of the Christian is to live in the light. I once had a leader who said to pretend everything you do will end up on the front page of the *New York Times*. God's way is not the world's way!

Once the chairman of the board of a $20-billion company interviewed me. On his desk was a ruler, upon which was written "Never let the pursuit of success compromise your integrity." That is how he conquered evil in his business, which led to the company's tremendous success!

Jesus, help me to be good to all, especially to those who seek evil for me. I praise You for conquering evil in my life.

How can you tell God how much His protection means to you? How can the Holy Spirit help you conquer evil in your life?

Romans 13:1 "Let every person be subordinate to the higher authorities, for there is no authority except from God, and those that exist have been established by God."

Jesus calls us to be humble in all aspects of our life. Sometimes humility is difficult when we do not get along with family members, friends, the boss or colleagues. We need God's grace to get us through. Don't give up! God's grace will bolster us through difficult moments. Jesus will us strengthen gently, teaching us humility.

Sometimes we find it difficult to respect our boss or others in authority. Remember, always submit to their authority to build up yourself and be a solid Christian witness.

Lord, I thank You for the person in authority that You chose especially for me.

How can you be an example of love for your family, friends, co-workers? God has given you many gifts to battle and reject evil. You must recognize what is not of God and discern when you are attacked. Do you ask for the gift of discernment?

February 1

1 Thessalonians 5:11 "...encourage one another and build one another up, as indeed you do."

As we awaken each morning, are we ready to support and build up each person whom we meet or with whom we work? So often, we think of only ourselves rather than the person standing right in front of us—family member, colleague, friend stranger. Yet, God's entire purpose for us is to spread His love to all we encounter.

One of the best compliments I have received is to be called an "encourager." Sometimes a single sentence or comment might impact someone's life for the positive forever. Ask to be used as an instrument of encouragement, and you will become that instrument.

Lord, open my eyes to see those who need encouragement and support today.

How can you make a difference for others? What positive actions you take or guiding words you speak can be used to make someone's day, whether a friend, loved one or co-worker? In doing this, you build up the Body of Christ.

Isaiah 54:17 "No weapon fashioned against you shall prevail;/ every tongue shall prove false/ that launches an accusation against you...."

In this world, many weapons can be launched against us. The good news is God will defeat them all! We need not be dismayed or discouraged. Call upon our Lord to protect and defend us!

I suggest you memorize today's Scripture to be used as a weapon against any evil attacking you, your family and your loved ones. God's Word is reality!

Lord, thank You for Your protection. Praise the name of Jesus!

Are there times when you feel attacked or sad, or that your joy has been compromised? Do you trust in the Lord to be your redeemer, healer, your omnipotent Lord? He is waiting to be asked! Do you allow Him to heal you with an open heart? What do you do in times of attack? Do you trust in Him or do you rely on yourself and then suffer because of denial of Jesus' healing power and grace?

1 Corinthians 14:40 "...but everything must be done properly and in order."

In everyday life, decisions must be made. Will the means justify the end? This verse doesn't leave room for options. Every action must be illuminated by the light of Christ. You may try to hide from family, friends, your boss or others, but you can never escape the scrutiny of God.

Seek the wisdom of the Lord on how to run your life, career or business in an organized and orderly manner. He will provide you a way to do it.

Lord, help me today and always to do everything properly and with the greatest integrity. I praise You for the grace of the gift of integrity.

Do you try your best in the daily routine of life; whether it is your job, work in the community, the church or your interactions at home? Do you glorify His name when you go about your day? How successful are you in achieving this goal?

Hebrews 4:16 "So let us confidently approach the throne of grace to receive mercy and to find grace for timely help."

To receive grace is to be in friendship with God. Do you have any better friend? Jesus knows that we need Him to live a life of peace and joy. When trials occur, we can ask God for help, and He will come to our aid always, especially when we need it the most!

One key to this verse is the word "approach." We can't obtain the grace God wants to give us unless we approach Him and ask for it!

Lord, help me to humble myself and ask for Your help when I am in the midst of life's trials. I praise You and thank You for the gift of grace!

Are there times when you are reluctant to ask for God's help? When you ask for help, do you praise Him and His infinite abilities or do you use Him as a "god of convenience"? How can you strengthen your love and relationship of trust in God? Ask the Holy Spirit to guide you.

Matthew 6:8b "Your Father knows what you need before you ask him."

Do you ever think someone can read your mind? Do they know what you are thinking and say it before you do? Perhaps it's your spouse or a close friend—someone with whom you share your intimate feelings. God knows the "real" you better than you know yourself or anyone else ever could. We never need to hide anything from Him because God already knows it.

When you pray to God with petitions, He knows what is best for you before you think of or even voice it. Ask Him, and if it is His will, you will be blessed even more!

Lord, thank you for knowing my needs before the dawn of time. I praise and thank you for being my best friend.

Do you trust God's perfect will? Do you allow yourself to trust in Him to know your thoughts, heart and needs? Do you understand that sometimes He says no, because He knows better? After all, He is "Our Father Who Art in Heaven." When have you trusted God—and when have you not?

Genesis 12:2 "'I will make you a great nation,/ and I will bless you;/ I will make your name great,/ so that you will be a blessing.'"

I received a word from the Lord that a great nation would be associated with a company of which I became President a few years ago. The great nation was the sales forces hired to sell pharmaceutical products. They were blessed with God's grace because we formed the company under His guidance and the direction of the Holy Spirit and for His glory. God's Word indeed bore fruit and the company became a nearly $100-million company in four years!

To be blessed means we have supernatural favor. We always receive that favor when we ask for it. Why? He will never deny us the Holy Spirit and the fruits of the Spirit.

Lord, thank you for helping me be part of building the Kingdom. I praise You for being the source of all blessings in my life.

Do you see the reward that results from following God in your life? Do you bear fruit in the name of Jesus?

Psalm 16:8 "I set the LORD ever before me;/ with him at my right hand I shall not be disturbed."

When we put God at the center of our lives, nothing can prevent God's love from filling us with His joy and peace. We trust God will supply all our needs, hopes and dreams. Nothing is more important than God's will in our lives.

Life can be complicated or simple. Jesus wants it simple! Trust in Him and be filled with His hope, peace, joy and love.

Today, Lord help me to put You first in everything I do. I praise you for giving me the gift of wisdom.

Do you stop during day to ask yourself if you are following His perfect will? Do you get so busy that you forget to follow God's ways and lose sight of your purpose? When have you put God first? Ask Him to help you recognize His infinite wisdom and to follow His way—the truth.

Proverbs 11:2 "When pride comes, disgrace comes;/ but with the humble is wisdom."

Pride is the root of all evil. It is also the basis of all failure. When we think we know best and want to control our lives, we prevent God from working through us. We block His miracles from being manifested in our lives because we fail to surrender to His power and love.

Most of us struggle with humility. We think it is weakness. Yet, Jesus was the humblest of all. He died on the cross, despite being God!

Lord, I praise You for the gift of humility and helping me to embrace it with all my heart.

When have you been prideful in your actions and have them backfire? How can you become more focused on Christ and more closely follow His selfless ways?

Philippians 4:4 "Rejoice in the Lord always. I say it again: rejoice!"

I find it interesting that Paul had to remind us twice to rejoice always, no matter what is occurring in our lives. We usually think of celebrating or rejoicing when something great happens—joyous occasions such as an anniversary or birthday. The world tells us to celebrate a job promotion or winning the lottery.

God's way is different. He wants us to celebrate the ordinary things in our life. God wants to pour out His supernatural blessings on us for all of eternity. For the "King's kids," it is better than winning the grand prize of the biggest lottery ever! All we must do is say "Yes!" and rejoice!

Lord; help me rejoice today in all things—both ordinary and amazing! I praise you for the gift of this day.

When things don't go your way, do you rejoice and thank God for what is His will? How do you show God how much you love and praise Him for all things in your life?

Ephesians 1:3 "Blessed be the God and Father of our Lord Jesus Christ, who has blessed us in Christ with every spiritual blessing in the heavens...."

Perhaps you have heard the phrase "having heaven on earth." I'm sure most of us wonder what heaven is like and don't want it to be like what we experience on earth. As Christians, we can experience heaven when we "touch the garment" of our Lord. Through prayer and praise, we enter into His presence and encounter tremendous joy and peace. We, indeed, receive the same blessings of heaven here on earth!

Meditate on this verse and ponder the power and blessings God is giving you today and forever.

Lord, I praise you for giving me blessings from heaven today. Help me to see them in all that I encounter.

Reflect on how many blessings are in your life, write them down, and praise God for them!

Revelation 3:15-16 "I know your works; I know that you are neither cold nor hot. I wish you either cold or hot. So, because you are lukewarm, neither hot nor cold, I will spit you out of my mouth."

This Scripture passage hits us right between the eyes! What do we believe in? What do we stand for—a little of everything? Whatever the boss says? Whatever is politically correct?

During wartime, we have to declare sides. We are in a war now, whether we realize it or not. If we don't declare for Jesus, we declare for the enemy by default. There is no middle ground. Sorry, like gravity, some rules cannot change. Where do you want to be counted? What side are you on?

Lord, today I declare my allegiance to you for eternity. Praise God forever!

How can you be bold in your faith? How do you show you will fight on and go to battle because of your faith and trust in the Lord?

1 Thessalonians 5:19 "Do not quench the Spirit."

One line—just five words. Yet this verse helps determine how much we help build the kingdom of God. If we don't embrace God with all our heart, then we are quenching the Spirit. If I am lukewarm in my faith, I limit the power of the Holy Spirit to work in my life.

We often don't realize how much we quench the Spirit by our actions.

Lord, today send forth the Holy Spirit as tongues of fire in my life; I praise you for gift of the Holy Spirit.

Today is the day that you claim your Baptism of the Holy Spirit! What gifts should you ask for? What gifts will you receive? Wait in anticipation and with excitement as you pray and discern the gifts God wishes to give you.

Isaiah 50:4 "The Lord GOD has given me/ a well-trained tongue,/ That I might know how to speak to the weary/ a word that will rouse them."

The use of words is one of our primary weapons in life. How we use them helps determine our success in all aspects of our life. This verse confirms that God will prepare us for what we need to say to His people. Frequently speak words of encouragement, support, protection and love with your family!

Don't ever fear speaking in front of a group or with someone ever again! Most of us don't like to speak in public. If we trust in the Lord and meditate on this verse, God will take over our talk. This was meant for you!

Lord, thank you for teaching me what to say to Your people today. I praise You for the gift of communication.

How will you use the God-given talents bestowed upon you to encourage people—by speaking the Truth of Jesus Christ's message from His Father?

1 Corinthians 13:4 "Love is patient, love is kind."

On Valentine's Day, it is only appropriate that we take a verse from the Bible's "love chapter." Being patient and kind summarizes love; the greatest of all gifts, it is the essence of God.

How difficult is it to be patient in your home or at work? Without patience, kindness usually evaporates. The good thing is that if we ask to love more, God always grants our request it by giving us patience and kindness.

Lord, help me today to love as You love. I praise You for being the God of love.

How can you begin to love better? Sometimes the ones closest to us are the hardest to love. How do you recapture the love for those you have neglected? Do you focus on His love of them? Is that not what you want to strive for?

Acts 3:26 "For you first, God raised up his servant and sent him to bless you by turning each of you from your evil ways."

I'm sure all of us, in examining our conscience over the past days and years, have asked ourselves honestly if we like who we are and how we are living our lives. Have we turned to Jesus with our whole heart, soul, mind and strength? Or do we just go through the motions? Do we really want all evil to be rooted out of our lives or only that part which feels safe?

When we totally submit to God, His blessings will flow like a river that does not end.

Lord, thank You for dying on the cross for us and giving us freedom from sin as we accept You as our Lord and Savior. I praise You for being my Savior.

Do you know in your heart that Jesus is your Savior? Do you believe He suffered and died for you? Do you realize how special you are to Him?

Matthew 10:39 "Whoever finds his life will lose it, and whoever loses his life for my sake will find it."

Most people in this world will do anything they can to feel important or significant. They buy houses, cars, clothes, etc. They earn many academic degrees to feel smart. Most live in dread that they will be found out as "lesser than."

God's way is completely different. It says we must not strive to be important, but to be humble, as Jesus was humble. We must surrender all pride so that He can fill us up with His love.

Jesus, help me today to surrender my life, so that You can fill me up with Your love. I praise You for the gift of faith, which helps me surrender to Your will.

Do you realize that being humble and surrendering your pride to God is a blessing and that your heart will be opened to even more grace?

2 Thessalonians 3:3 "But the Lord is faithful; he will strengthen you and guard you from the evil one."

No matter what we do today, God will be faithful to us. Did we start the day with praise and thanksgiving or with grumbling? Did we curse our job or neighbor? Or did we encourage those we encountered? God will always be faithful even if we are not. He will always respect our wishes. If we don't want Him in our lives, He won't force Himself on us.

When we pray the "Our Father," we ask God to protect us from evil and our adversaries. Jesus delivers 100% of the time.

Lord, thank You for Your faithfulness. Help me to remember You today and to ask for Your protection. I praise You for being my protector for eternity!

Do you trust in God to deliver all evil from your life? When has there been a time when you should have asked Him for help, but didn't? If you trust in Him, turn your gaze to the Lord when you feel afraid.

Luke 9:25 "What profit is there for one to gain the whole world yet lose or forfeit himself?"

Life is about choices. Psychologists tell us we make more than 2,000 choices per day. We can choose to love, to follow Jesus, or not. We can choose the world and its temporary riches and pleasures or we can choose eternal happiness.

In business and with other things of our life, temptations abound in the pursuit of success. Many times, we are tempted to do whatever it takes to win at life and business. However, if we fall to that lie, we have lost the battle—we forsake our soul. True success comes from following Jesus.

Lord Jesus, I choose You today to follow for eternity. I praise You for showing me what is "true success."

His truth is all you need to bring eternal peace. How do you seek His truth and light in your life?

Mark 12:17 "…'Repay to Caesar what belongs to Caesar and to God what belongs to God.'"

It is getting close to tax season and complaining begins. Haven't I paid too much tax already? Isn't the tax code unfair? The basis of all sin is pride, and the basis of pride is rationalization. It is very simple with God. Everything we have is His and for His glory. God has appointed authorities over us, which we must respect and give what is required. He is giving directs us to give a fitting portion of our monies to the government, according to the rules of the state. It is called obedience and discipline, which leads to discipleship

Lord, help me put my finances in proper alignment with your will. I praise you for being the source of honesty.

Do you use your resources to glorify God's name? When do you? When don't you? How can you change your ways when you feel the temptation to use money to dishonor your name?

Jeremiah 17:14 "Heal me, LORD, that I may be healed;/ save me, that I may be saved,/ for it is you, whom I praise."

All of us experience hurts and wounds, starting from the moment we are born! We come from God and, as believers, will return to Him. In the middle of our existence, our time on Earth, we are often wounded and in pain. We may need a doctor for physical hurts or someone to help with spiritual healing. As we pray and worship, we begin the healing process by reuniting with God.

As children of God, we are people of praise and healing—both for the community and ourselves. We are freed from sin and illness and given the grace to love and live abundantly.

Lord, I need to be healed. I praise and thank You for being my healer and redeemer.

God in His infinite wisdom and knowledge knows what healing is needed in your life. When you listen to the Lord, do you acknowledge what healing you need so you can better serve Him?

Psalm 116:17 "To you will I offer sacrifice of thanksgiving,/ and I will call upon the name of the LORD."

What does the Psalmist mean by a sacrifice of Thanksgiving? How can I make it part of my daily activities?

If we praise God for all things, we make a sacrifice for prayer and thanksgiving to God for everything. In so doing, we are calling upon Him to come into our life and take over.

Lord, I praise You for all things today!

What are the daily blessings in your life that you need to praise God for?

Isaiah 46:10 "At the beginning I foretell the outcome/ in advance, things not yet done./ I say that my plan shall stand,/ I accomplish my every purpose."

How many times have you put together a personal or business plan, only to have it change almost immediately? Perhaps, you have heard the saying, "We plan, God laughs."

Most of us believe our success in life is based on our talent. While planning is important, listening is the critical priority. God will show us what to do through prayer, counsel from other Christians or the Bible, etc. We must adjust our plans according to what God is telling us to do. Often, He is telling us to stand our ground and not to be discouraged.

Lord, fashion my plans for your glory and for the good of your people. I praise you for being the source of my wisdom.

How do you quiet your mind? Pray fervently in contemplative prayer so that you hear the Father's words? Where is there a place of peace for you to sit, be still and listen to His perfect will and loving message?

Luke 21:19 "By your perseverance you will secure your lives."

Winners never quit, and quitters never win. As Christians, we always win when we don't give up. There are so many times, when we feel like giving up. Things are not going according to our plans, so discouragement sets in. A friend of mine taught me that "expectations are premeditated resentment." Expect God's grace—not our own plan of success.

God calls us to be faithful, not successful! Satan wins only if I fail to persevere. When I repent of trying to control my life, I win! Then, God is free to work His plan for my life through me.

Lord, thank you for giving me your Holy Spirit and the gift of perseverance. I praise You for teaching me that surrendering to you is the source of true success.

When have you given up on the Lord? How can you show your trust in God, leaning on Him and seeking His guidance through difficult and trying times?

Luke 14:11 "For everyone who exalts himself will be humbled, but the one who humbles himself will be exalted."

If you ever wonder how much you desire being the center of attention, look at your behavior for just one day. What do you say or do that centers on just yourself rather than on others? Do you enjoy getting recognition, being admired or even put on a pedestal? Resist the temptation, because God's way is not the world's approach. When we are meek, we are strong in God's eyes. We will be blessed with His grace. As we seek to put others first, our humility will be blessed for all eternity.

Lord, help me humble myself today with all that I do. I praise you for being the source of humility.

How can you feel humble before the Lord? Prayers for humility and the recognition that God is the source of all power will guide you to a humbler way of life.

Nehemiah 8:9 "...'Today is holy to the LORD your God. Do not be sad, and do not weep'...."

Each day that we live is holy before God, a blessing, because God has said everything He created is good. It is not for us to be sad or despondent. We are to rejoice in this day of holiness, as we reflect upon the beauty of His creation and wonder of His people.

When people see us or hear our voices, they should see that we are different. They should see that we are God's sons and daughters, joyful and full of love.

Lord, thank You for this holy day. Help me to praise Your name throughout the day.

Are you thankful for the Lord's miracles of each day? Do you express your gratitude and remember all that is good in your life comes from God?

Numbers 22:12 "...'Do not go with them and do not curse this people, for they are blessed.'"

It is important to remember that the people we encounter have their own relationship with God. They are sons and daughters of our Creator and need to be treated as such. I have often said that we should treat each person as the queen or king of England.

We meet God's children daily, and in each of them, we may even be entertaining angels! As we bless God's people, so shall we receive His blessings!

Lord, give me the grace to bless all I meet with or talk to today. I praise you for being the source of all blessings.

Are you sometimes negative or judgmental in your thinking about others? Who is that one person about whom you just can't seem to find anything positive? Reflect upon how this person is also a child of God; because He honors them, so must you. Focus on their talents and positive attributes to help you change your attitude towards them.

Psalm 107:20 "He sent forth his word to heal them/ and to snatch them from destruction."

How can God's Word heal? We know that Jesus is the incarnate Word that dwells among His people. He is light, life and truth. The Bible is a love letter to us from Jesus. It gives us guidance, support and comfort, leading to our healing.

When we are headed down the wrong path, Jesus is always there. All we need to do is ask and He will turn us around. So ask him today! Jesus is our comforter and redeemer.

Lord; help me to turn to your Bible in time of need to receive your healing presence in my life.

Is it difficult for you to crack open the Bible? Have you tried to read passages, but just don't understand them? Do you hear His messages in the Bible? Do you explore your faith in the Bible? How can you make the Bible a daily event?

Matthew 5:8 "Blessed are the clean of heart,/ for they will see God."

In the Old Testament, we learn from Psalms that only the pure in heart can participate in temple worship. It means to behold the face of God.

In the Beatitudes, the Christian experiences God now and in the "kingdom to come." We, the soldiers of Christ, can begin to see God as we purify our lives during the routine of our daily activities. When we are pure of heart, we can see God much more clearly. His presence becomes very real to us.

Lord, I seek your face today! Purify my heart. I praise the Sacred Heart of Jesus.

Do you recognize Jesus in the hearts of others and in your own heart? Do you seek His face? Reflect on your first meeting with Jesus in heaven and imagine His holy face. How glorious He is!

Acts 13:3 "Then, completing their fasting and prayer, they laid hands on them and sent them off."

As a leader in life or business, there is a great responsibility to be honest and truthful in all things. We must also put the needs of others first—before anything else.

It is often difficult to be patient with others; however, it is still important to be both a coach and an encourager. That is what the Lord wants from us!

Lord, give me Your strength to pray and fast for the people I know and encounter. Give me the wisdom to release them to be led by you. I praise you Jesus, for being Lord of my life.

Are you an encourager of the people in your life? Do you listen to God's prompting on how to accomplish this?

March 1

Mark 16:18 "...'They will lay hands on the sick, and they will recover.'"

God heals! He heals us spiritually, mentally, emotionally and physically. Do you know what it means to be filled by the Holy Spirit? It is total and complete surrender to His presence.

When you do this, Jesus takes over your life and you become a new creation. It is no longer you, but Christ in you. Then you can do what Christ desires: help His people. This includes listening, loving and being an instrument of healing in any way that Christ deems necessary.

Lord, give me your grace and miraculous powers so that your love may flow through me to your people. I praise you for being my healer.

Do you recognize God's healing power in your life and others? How do you let His love flow through you and allow God to heal you?

Jeremiah 20:11 "But the LORD is with me, like a mighty champion:/ my persecutors will stumble, they will not triumph./ In their failure they will be put to utter shame,/ to lasting, unforgettable confusion."

How would you like to have God as your mighty champion? Do you believe it is possible? Is anything impossible with the Creator of the universe?

Know that God is blessing you, is with you and is keeping you from harm. When you follow God's will, your personal champion will stop principalities and/or other powers in their tracks. Call upon Him!

Lord, thank you for being my champion. Help me today to increase my faith so that I will trust and follow only You. I praise God for being the source of all that is good in my life.

Do you tell the Lord how much you love Him and how you love growing in faith? Praise God from the depths of your heart!

Isaiah 45:3 "I will give you treasures out of the darkness,/ and riches that have been hidden away,/ That you may know that I am the LORD,/ the God of Israel, who calls you by name."

Have you ever received God's blessings when you least expected? Perhaps it was a beautiful sunset, a friend who suddenly appeared out of the blue to share encouraging words, or the feel of God's love when you needed it the most. Jesus wants us to receive His blessings and treasures.

I believe His blessings and love are often found in the area of our greatest difficulty. It is part of the reason why we need to praise Him for all things.

Lord, I thank You for calling me by name. Help me to recognize the treasures You have for me. I praise You for being my friend, my advocate, my source.

Are you looking for your blessings from God each day? Are your eyes and mind open to them?

Proverbs 21:3 "To do what is right and just/ is more acceptable to the LORD than sacrifice."

There are times when we think God wants us to give up everything in our lives we find enjoyable. This is a lie from the enemy to keep us from a holier life with God.

Jesus only wants us to put Him first before anything else, including our families. This is because God doesn't want idol worship. By surrendering to Him all that we are and have, the joy of the Lord is released in our lives. The truth of this surrender is we don't give up anything important, but get everything in return.

Lord, thank You for teaching me that You desire not only my sacrifice, but also my heart. I praise You for being my teacher.

What in life do you sacrifice to God? Do you offer God your whole life, heart, soul, mind and body? Do you listen to God's wisdom and teachings? When do you fail in this?

Matthew 5:34 "But I say to you, do not swear at all...."

How bad is swearing? Isn't it acceptable in today's culture, at work or in our personal environment? No! Jesus demands holiness.

We are to be pure in thought, word and speech.

God's ways are not the world's ways. If we swear, we are serving notice that God is not within our speech and that we are in the flesh.

Jesus, help me to set the right example by taking over my speech. I praise You for being the example of all purity.

How do you feel when you offend the Lord? Do you realize He is offended by your harmful words? Who do you hurt in your life with harsh words?

John 16:24 "Until now you have not asked anything in my name; ask and you will receive, so that your joy may be complete."

Jesus tells His disciples repeatedly that they are to ask the Father anything and they will get it. For us, such instruction may not appear to make sense or be feasible. We pray, but our prayers are not always answered. Is it a lack of faith? Was this direction meant only for the apostles? No! Our prayers are not answered as we want because we do not ask "in the name of Jesus." When we do so, we ask in the "will" of Jesus. Indeed, Jesus cannot deny himself.

Remember it is impossible to please God without faith. Faith as big as a mustard seed will move the mountains in your life.

Lord, help me touch your garment as I surrender in faith to Your will in my life and with those I pray for. I praise You for being the source of all faith in my life.

How do you look to God to gain more faith? When do you use your faith for convenience? How can you trust in God and be more faithful?

March 7

Genesis 18:14 "Is anything too marvelous for the LORD to do?"

Nothing can ever be better than the Lord's generosity. Let Him show you! Ask Him to heal you and your family. Allow Jesus to be CEO of your job or business. Know that with God, all things are possible.

Do you believe? Today, God wants to do miracles in your life and that of your family. Trust in Him and He will act!

One of the greatest miracles in our lives, Katie, was born on this day. She is an example of God's love for us. He sent her to help us edit this book of praise and launch our Evangelization and Healing Ministry, "Spirit Filled Hearts."

Lord, thank you for your blessings and increasing my faith today. I praise you for all that you do in my life and for being my Savior, my redeemer and my deliverer.

When do you praise God in your life? How has praising the Lord made your faith increase?

Isaiah 52:7 "How beautiful upon the mountains/ are the feet of him who brings glad tidings,/ Announcing peace, bearing good news,/ announcing salvation...."

We are the fulfillment of this passage. God wants us to go into the world and announce His Good News of salvation, the best tidings anyone could ever receive. Our lives and jobs are vehicles to proclaim the love and salvation of Christ in the world. If no one had told you the Good News, you wouldn't be as far along in your faith as you are today. God is depending on you to do the same for His people.

Lord, help me to use my life, my job and ministries as tools to build up your kingdom on earth. I praise you for the gift of evangelism.

When and how do you evangelize? Do you evangelize through your actions, spoken words of testimony or maybe by sharing your faith?

March 9

Matthew 6:10 "...your kingdom come,/ your will be done,/ on earth as in heaven.

Most of us think heaven is far from our existence on Earth. One thing is consistent: the will of the Father will be fulfilled now and forever. Our purpose in life is to make a decision to accept His will. By doing so, we will be in His presence for eternity.. If you pray for the Lord's will to permeate your life, He will transform you!

I praise You Lord for having Your will part of me now and forever.

Is your faith deep enough that you trust in God's will? How can you improve in your faith journey by trusting His will?

March 10

Nehemiah 8:10 "...'Go, eat rich foods, and drink sweet drinks, and allot portions to those who had nothing prepared; for today is holy to our LORD. Do not be saddened this day, for rejoicing in the LORD must be your strength."

There are days when we feel the weight of the world on our shoulders. Finances, spouse, children, etc., can be all-consuming. God doesn't want us to be sad or to feel down. He wants a smile on our face, laughter in our voice and joy in our heart. We are children of His kingdom. Act as if we believe it, and we will be blessed. With the King's kids, all things are possible.

Lord, I praise you for giving the gift of rejoicing now and forever.

There are so many gifts and blessings in your life. Recognize them and praise God!

Romans 8:18 "I consider the sufferings of this present time are as nothing compared with the glory to be revealed for us."

God's grace is infinitely beyond the suffering of the present life. We know that suffering is part of life. However, when we turn our heart to Jesus we receive His love, joy and fruit of the Holy Spirit. Christ's redemption is the basis of all joy, leading to future glory and eternal happiness. We must focus on Jesus while riding on this roller coaster called life. He will take our burdens and trade them for peace every time.

Read again the promise of today's scripture passage. God is here to bless us today and forever. Suffering will go away, but God's grace stays forever.

Lord, thank You for helping me through this day. I hope to spend eternal life with You. I praise You as my Savior.

Do you stop and praise God during the day? How do you realize His daily miracles that help you to know just a glimmer of the eternal life He offers you?

Isaiah 58:6-7 "This, rather, is the fasting that I wish:/ releasing those bound unjustly,/ untying the thongs of the yoke;/ Sharing your bread with the hungry,/ sheltering the oppressed and the homeless; Clothing the naked when you see them, and not turning your back on your own."

We will never surrender completely to God's will if we can't show compassion and care for the poor and oppressed. Jesus wants us to be very active in taking care of His people. We must never turn our back to them at any time. What does that mean for our daily living? God will provide the answers when you ask. Remember, God will not give you guilt or condemn you, but He will be truthful when you fall short of His will for His people.

Lord, help me today to be an instrument of help and peace for Your people. I praise You for being my prince of peace.

Do you recognize all of God's children as fellow members of the Body of Christ? Do you notice the less fortunate? Do you recognize them in your life? When do you serve them?

Habakkuk 2:3 "For the vision still has its time,/ presses on to fulfillment, and will not disappoint;/ If it delays, wait for it,/ it will surely come, it will not be late."

God always keeps His promises in the fullness of time. He will never disappoint. We, who are in the flesh, often expect it to be on our time schedule and when we want it—like a baby crying for its milk.

Wanting what we don't have, when we want it, is called lust. We want instant gratification. If this occurs to us, we must repent immediately!

Lord, thank You for Your patience and helping me see Your hand in every aspect of my life. I praise You for being my source of patience.

Do you treasure the gifts God has given you? What gifts from God do you recognize in your life?

March 14

Malachi 3:10 "Bring the whole tithe/ into the storehouse,/ That there may be food in my house,/ and try me in this, says the LORD of hosts;/ Shall I not open for you the floodgates of heaven,/ to pour down blessings upon you without measure?"

We are stewards of all of God's gifts, including financial. Knowing how to use God's money is an important part of our Christian walk.

We must remember that all our money is God's money, and that we are its safe-keepers. Therefore, we need to give Him the first fruits of our labor. When we do that, without expectation, God will bless us without reservation. We will not need or want for anything truly important in our life.

Lord, thank You for taking care of me in every way, including my finances. I praise You for being the source of my finances and giving me the gift of generosity.

Do you attribute your financial gains to your gifts from God or do you attribute it all to your own hard work, talents and efforts?

Isaiah 43: 19 "See, I am doing something new! / Now it springs forth, do you not perceive it?/ In the desert, I make a way,/ the in the wasteland, rivers."

We are a new creation in Christ Jesus! Can you feel it? Don't worry; faith has nothing to do with feeling. However, we should see the growth of joy, peace, patience and all the fruits of the Holy Spirit in our lives. We strive to grow in holiness each day.

The living waters of Jesus are cleansing our lives, which had been dominated by sin. Do not be discouraged by your daily activities. See the whole picture of what Jesus is doing in your life and rejoice!

Jesus, I rejoice in being a new creation in You! Thank You for Your blessings. I praise You for creating, for me, a new wineskin.

How do you praise the Lord for His creating within you a new sense of joy?

1 Peter 2:24 "He himself bore our sins in his body upon the cross, so that, free from sin, we might live for righteousness. By his wounds you have been healed."

In the season of Lent, it is important to reflect on the power and love of the cross. Why did Jesus die for us? Because He loves us individually. He purified us with His blood.

We have been healed of all our physical, mental, emotional and spiritual wounds. Rejoice and be glad!

Thank You Lord, for the indescribable gift of dying on the cross for our sins and the healing of our wounds. I praise You for being my Savior!

How do you show your gratitude for Jesus' death on the cross? Every day do you feel thankful for His incredible love?

Deuteronomy 4:31 "Since the LORD, your God, is a merciful God, he will not abandon and destroy you, nor forget the covenant which under oath he made with your fathers."

Even when we forget about God, He doesn't forget us. He is there blessing us, if we are open to it.

Jesus will heal us, forgive us and help us. All we need do is ask. Jesus never remembers our sins when we sincerely confess them to Him. Rejoice in His great mercy and receive His love.

Lord, I praise and thank You for never forgetting or abandoning me.

What in your life affects your ability to praise and love God? How grateful are you that He continues to love you!

Matthew 14:31 "Immediately Jesus stretched out his hand and caught him, and said to him, 'O you of little faith, why did you doubt?'"

Why do we doubt? Why do we have so little faith when we have received so many of God's blessings? Why do we think it will stop? My wife reminds me often that Jesus has always taken care of me in the past and will in the future.

Our flesh can be very weak at times, so we doubt and mistrust. Jesus tells us what is needed is trust and faith. We know that perfect love casts out all fear. That perfect love comes from Jesus.

Lord, open my eyes to see how You support in my darkest moments. I praise You for being my healer and protector.

Look into your heart. Have you failed to feel and recognize God's great love and support during life's trials? When you ignore His love, you block His grace from coming into your life. Turn your heart over to Him.

March 19

Luke 5:10 "...'Do not be afraid; from now on you will be catching men.'"

I feel very blessed because God gave me this Scripture verse for my life after a prayer session with Him. If we are open to His calling, He will shower us with His many blessings.

Along with these blessings comes a great responsibility—responsibility for ministering to and helping souls enter into the kingdom of God. We don't save souls—God does—but, when asked by God, we must proclaim that Jesus is the way, the truth and the life.

Lord, open my heart, to receive Your vision of "catching" men and women for Your kingdom. I praise You for choosing me as your voice in the wilderness.

When you open your heart to God, how do you feel His great joy? His love flows through you when you proclaim God's Good News to His people through evangelization.

Psalm 40:4 "And he put a new song into my mouth,/ a hymn to our God./ Many shall look on in awe/ and trust in the LORD."

Sing to the Lord a new song! Sing to the Lord a new song!

The Psalmist is referring to the transformation from lamentation to praise.

When we sing to God, we pray twice. When we praise God, especially in song, we truly please Him. It is important to make an effort to praise His name in song, as often as possible.

Lord, open my heart to sing a new song to You daily! I praise You for being the song that is always in my heart, longing for You.

Praising God brings such great joy; how do you share that joy daily?

Acts 27:24 "...'Do not be afraid, Paul. You are destined to stand before Caesar; and behold, for your sake, God has granted safety to all who are sailing with you."

Do you ever watch a tape of a sporting event when you know your team wins? I am a huge UCLA fan (don't hold that against me), and I have seen their NCAA championship game against Arkansas 10-plus times. I know who wins, but I still get nervous when they aren't doing well. However, it is only for a second, because I know those jump shots will begin falling.

That's the way our life should be. In the end, we win with Jesus. If things aren't going well at the moment, they will be soon, because God takes care of His children.

Thank You Lord for showing me that my life will end victoriously. I praise You for the victory over evil.

Do you trust in His ways, that He will help bring you to His heaven and everlasting life?

Acts 10:4 "...'Your prayers and almsgiving have ascended as a memorial offering before God.'"

Our prayers are like sweet incense before the Lord. They are a sweet fragrance that reaches heaven's chambers.

If we truly understood the importance of prayer, we would make it the center of our lives. Never forget how many souls are in conflict with sin and need your prayers to assist them in their pursuit of God.

Lord, help me today pray for those in most need of Your mercy. I praise You for the gift of praise and intercessory prayer.

How do you pray for other people to receive God's mercy? Your prayers for others are powerful! This type of prayer is selfless and makes you obtain the image of Christ.

Psalm 91:10 "No evil shall befall you,/ nor shall affliction come near your tent."

Rejoice! This is supreme protection from the Lord! He wants to protect us from all evil. We do not need fear anything or anybody. For if God is for us, who can be against us?

God protects us by loving us unconditionally—just as we are. No one can prevail against that.

Lord, I thank and praise You for your protection and for surrounding us with Your angels.

How do you recognize the love and blessings God gives you by providing you with your own guardian angel? How do you feel God protects you from harm?

Psalm 27:1 "The LORD is my light and my salvation;/ whom should I fear?/ The LORD is my life's refuge;/ of whom should I be afraid?"

God's presence is all around us. If we look through spiritual eyes, we would see angels in battle, protecting us from evil.

We would see the Holy Spirit, hovering in our midst.

It is the Lord's desire for us to be with Him in heaven. All we need to do is say "Yes." In our saying "Yes," we allow the Lord to remove all fear from our lives.

Lord, thank You for saving me and removing all fear from my life, now and forever. I praise You for being my Savior.

Do you thank God for blessing you with His grace, which protects you from fear?

Matthew 11:29 "Take my yoke upon you and learn from me, for I am meek and humble of heart; and you will find rest for yourselves."

Jesus wants us to be His students. He wants to teach us how to get through life with His grace. We must surrender our lives to Him and rest in Him. Much as a baby surrenders to its mother and is fed by her, Jesus wants to us to be nourished by Him. How much does anxiety play a role in our lives? Jesus wants to remove all anxiety from our lives. Trust in Him and He will act!

Lord, teach me how to live my life and give me the humility to accept Your love and grace. I praise You for being the source of my grace.

How do you practice humility in your life? When have you failed?

Galatians 5:22-23 "In contrast, the fruit of the Spirit is love, joy, peace, patience, kindness, generosity, faithfulness, gentleness, self control. Against such there is no law."

The fruits of the Holy Spirit are the basis of all Christian life. If we are growing spiritually, we are growing in these areas, too.

It is a process.

At times, we can make great progress, and, at other times, we fail. However, in general, we should be moving forward or we need an examination of conscience and repentance.

Lord, I praise and thank You for Your fruits and the blessings of the Holy Spirit.

How do you thank God for using your fruits of the Holy Spirit? Do you build up His Kingdom in gratitude?

Matthew 6:13 "...and do not subject us to the final test,/ but deliver us from the evil one."

The Lord's Prayer teaches us how to pray. One element of this critical prayer that I had not reflected on until recently is the phrase "to be delivered from temptation"—that is, the "evil one." Often, my focus has been to stand and not fall when my flesh tempts me. However, God doesn't even want us to experience "the temptation." Why fight a battle that you don't have to? We win automatically if there is nothing to fight against.

Lord, thank You for delivering me from all temptations today. Lord, I praise You for protecting me against all evil.

Do you listen to God during the day? Do you recognize His words of wisdom that help you avoid failing and succumbing to temptations?

Psalm 138:8 "The LORD will complete what he has done for me;/ your kindness, O LORD, endures forever;/ forsake not the work of your hands."

All of us want to be successful; this Psalm is helpful and should be repeated often. Whatever ministry God is calling us to will be completed by Him if we ask Him to lead our efforts. This is the kind of success that God has planned.

Does this mean we won't have success in the world?

Absolutely not! It only means that your focus cannot be on worldly success but on the treasure in heaven for the kingdom.

I praise and thank You Lord, for completing the purpose that You have begun through me.

How do you praise God and fulfill His perfect will in your life?

Matthew 26:75 "…'Before the cock crows you will deny me three times.'"

This verse cuts straight to the heart. We reflect on Jesus' death on the cross. It is sobering to realize that our sins put Jesus on the cross. It is our denying of Him over and over again that led to His pain.

I can never love Him enough for forgiving my sins, as He forgave Peter, for taking on my sins and redeeming me.

Lord, help me never to forget how much You love me for all of eternity. I praise You for being my Savior and Redeemer.

Reflect each night a daily examination of conscience. During the course of the day, when did you move toward Christ or move away from Him?

John 19:38 "After this, Joseph of Arimathea, secretly a disciple of Jesus for fear of the Jews, asked Pilate if he could remove the body of Jesus. And Pilate permitted it. So he came and took his body."

God honors both the largest and smallest of the things we do for Him. Probably, most people don't think of this verse in the Bible as one of any significance. I do. The reason is because in the darkest of times, Joseph of Arimathea stood up and was counted for his faith in Jesus. He said he believed, no matter the cost.

Another important thing is that God wants us to do the "ordinary." Taking care of burial duties is a part of life. Don't think God is necessarily calling you to go to a faraway ministry. He may want you to do daily, ordinary and unspectacular tasks for Him.

Lord, teach me to follow Your will in the ordinary things of each day. I praise You for Your guidance.

Are you listening to the Lord's guidance in your life? How?

John 20:19 "On the evening of that first day of the week, when the doors were locked, where the disciples were, for fear of the Jews, Jesus came and stood in their midst and said to them, 'Peace be with you.'"

Isn't the disciples' fear typical of the way most of us would act? The apostles had just spent all their time in Jesus' presence, witnessing His many miracles in their lives and everywhere else, and they are locked in a room, afraid. Just as I have been in the past—afraid of the future, afraid some person would do something to upset me. It is called fear and depression and it's not of the Lord.

Lord, take away any fear of the future. Help me to have faith.

How do you let God conquer your fear? Lift your fears up to the Lord and let Him heal you!

Matthew 28:5 "Then the angel said to the women in reply, 'Do not be afraid! I know that you are seeking Jesus the crucified.'"

Many times, "people" serve as angels for us. Also, I strongly believe that many of us entertain angels without ever realizing it.

In both cases, we receive similar messages. Because we love Jesus, because we are seeking Him, we need not be afraid. Jesus is going before us to prepare for us His Kingdom. He takes on our cares and burdens because He loves us.

I thank and praise You Lord for sending us angels to watch over us and assure us not to be afraid.

What would you like to say to your guardian angel? How can you thank your angel for always being there for you? How can you develop a relationship with your guardian angel?

Luke 23:43 "...'Amen, I say to you, today you will be with me in Paradise.'"

Depressed? Discouraged? Disappointed? This verse is meant for you. The thief on the cross demonstrated his faith in Jesus and was saved on the spot. As we demonstrate our faith, we are also saved from the burdens of the day. Jesus enters our hearts and gives us his Holy Spirit in a more powerful way. Today will be like Paradise when we surrender to Him.

Lord, I surrender my life to You. Fill me with Your presence. I praise Your holy name.

Do you believe God will save you at the hour of your death, despite your past sins? When you repent, do you ask wholeheartedly for forgiveness and do you forgive yourself as God has? Do you believe you are forgiven?

Luke 24:16 "...but their eyes were prevented from recognizing him."

When we have sin in our lives or haven't been given the grace to behold the presence of the Lord, we are veiled from the spiritual truths that surround us. Have you ever reflected on a particular circumstance and looked at it differently? More as God might see it?

When that happens, know that God has lifted away part of your veil Rejoice!

Lord, open my eyes that I may see You more clearly. I praise You for being the source of my spiritual vision.

When you pray, do you see with Christ's vision or your own? What clouds your vision of His truth and light?

Luke 24:53 "...and they were continually in the temple praising God."

How do you tap into God's power in your life? How do you get more love, grace and peace?

I believe the keys are prayer and praise. After Jesus ascended into heaven, what was next for the apostles? Luke tells us, in the last verse of his gospel, that the apostles' highest priority was to be together in church, praising God. And, as St. Augustine said, "When we "sing" praise, we pray twice."

Lord, I love You. I live to praise Your name more each day.

Do you desire to praise God for the many blessings you have received in your life?

April 5

Romans 12:6 "Since we have gifts that differ according to the grace given to us, let us exercise them..."

Unfortunately, many of us look at others' gifts and feel inadequate. Why can't we sing, teach, lector, etc., as they can? What is wrong with me? Am I not blessed like they are?

The truth is that you have blessings equal to every Christian whoever lived on the planet, but just "different" gifts. Often, we don't recognize them because we are too busy coveting others' gifts and playing victim.

Today I also celebrate a precious gift I have received from the Lord; today is my wonderful, loving brother's birthday!

Lord, open my eyes to see the blessings and gifts You have given me. Help me to use them to build Your kingdom. I praise You for Your gifts.

What are your gifts? How can you use them in your life to make a positive change for the world, and to glorify God?

Jeremiah 33:3 "Call to me, and I will answer you; I will tell to you things great beyond reach of your knowledge."

One of my favorite stories concerns St. Joan of Arc. I don't know if this actually happened, but I believe it could have.

When Joan was brought before the Queen of France, she was asked why God was speaking to a lowly peasant girl, but rather than to the Queen of France. Joan answered respectfully, but truthfully, "Your highness, God is speaking to you also, but you aren't listening."

I love that story because it is so true. God speaks to us all day long. He speaks to us in our dreams, through Scripture and other people, and in every other way possible. But, to hear His whisper, we must be silent before Him. Then, He can guide our life.

Thank You Lord, for teaching me Your wisdom and knowledge. I praise You for being the source of my wisdom.

Do you carefully listen to God's words of wisdom in your heart? How can you listen better and follow through on living God's perfect will?

Jeremiah 32:27 "I am the LORD, the God of all mankind! Is anything impossible to me?"

Do you put God in a box? Do you believe that the Creator of the universe is still capable of doing anything—that He is omnipotent?

My friend loves to say that God has an infinite number of solutions for our problems, but needs only one. Do you think that the solution to our problems is beyond His ability?

What is needed more than ever in today's world is faith, faith to let God be God and to perform His miracles in our lives.

Bless me today, Lord, by giving me increased faith to believe that all things are possible through Your love. I praise You for the gift of faith.

Do you recognize the possibilities of miracles in your life? Do you trust Him with your whole life? When do you succeed and when do you fail in doing so?

Mark 1:11 "...'You are my beloved Son; with you I am well pleased.'"

Do we believe God is pleased with us? Is this verse only talking about Jesus and how the Father is pleased with only Him? I don't think so.

I know God wants us to love Him with all our heart, soul and might. When we do this, the Father is "also" very pleased with "us." He is not keeping score, but does look at the purity of our heart.

Lord, open my heart to serve You and to humble myself to receive Your blessings. I praise Your holy name, now and forever!

What in your soul needs to be made clean so that you can receive His blessings?

Matthew 12:33 "'Either declare the tree good and its fruit is good, or declare the tree rotten and its fruit is rotten, for a tree is known by its fruit.'"

What kind of tree are you? What kind of fruit is your life bearing? A good exercise is to ask yourself a simple question: is my life building up the kingdom of God or tearing it down? Our lives are not black and white. As Mother Teresa once said, "We are all capable of much good and much evil." However, if a little of our fruit is rotten, we can cut it out through God's grace. Be careful that the whole tree doesn't go past the point where it must be cut down.

Lord, help me today reflect on how much good fruit is manifested by my actions. I praise You for helping me to bear good fruit.

How is the fruit that you are given by God building up His people?

Jeremiah 29:11, "For I know well the plans I have in mind for you, says the LORD, plans for your welfare, not for woe! Plans to give you a future full of hope."

The Lord gave me this verse twice in my life. Both times it was regarding our moving from California to the East Coast. We would be moving away from our family, friends "and" our comfort zone. It was very frightening. However, I was convinced both times, and I still am, that we were meant to move back East for our personal growth and to help build the kingdom.

Jesus did come to our aid and got us back home, both times, in a timely manner—not without trials and tribulations, but with grace and hope

Lord, I thank and praise You for blessing me and filling my future with Your hope and Your grace. I love You!

How do you place your trust in God and know He takes care of your loved ones each day?

April 11

2 Timothy 2:19 "...'Let everyone who calls upon the name of the Lord avoid evil.'"

God will give us the strength to avoid all evil when we truly turn to Him with all of our heart. He wants to make it happen. Let Him, by saying "Yes!"

In some areas of our lives we struggle with sin. We often revisit these struggling areas when we are feeling depressed or things aren't going as we planned. Do you want a spiritual breakthrough? Give those areas to Jesus for healing. He will give you far more peace and joy than your temporary pleasures could ever provide.

Lord, I say yes to You for Your help in avoiding all sin and evil in my life. I praise and thank You for blessing and protecting me.

What evil is attacking you in your life? When do you call upon the Lord for His assistance? Do you ask for help and protection in the name of Jesus? Do you thank Him for His help?

Song of Songs 2:11-12 "For see, the winter is past,/ the rains are over and gone./ The flowers appear on the earth,/ the time of pruning the vines has come,/ and the song of the dove is heard in our land."

I believe success in life is as much about persistence as it is about anything else. It's easy to get discouraged about our progress or lack of it. God doesn't want us to focus on progress. He wants us to trust and believe. If He tells you that things will work out for His glory, then believe it. What is needed is trust. When that occurs, what had been "winter" will turn into the "spring" of new life in your life, work and family.

I praise You for being the God of hope and for giving me strength to endure my trials.

During hard times, do you doubt your faith or do you praise God for His enduring love and support for you?

Genesis 26:12-13 "Isaac sowed a crop in that region and reaped a hundredfold the same year. Since the LORD blessed him, he became richer and richer all the time, until he was very wealthy indeed."

When we devote our lives to the Lord, we sow a crop for Him. If we stay focused on serving Him, He will bless us abundantly. Do you believe it? Isaac did and was rewarded for it 100 times over. In the same way, we will be rewarded with God's blessings when we serve Him. It might be worldly riches, but more likely, it will be the fruits of the Holy Spirit.

Jesus, help me today to sow a crop for your kingdom. I praise and thank You for Your many blessings.

When do you tend your garden of faith? Do you pray throughout the day? How can you improve your devotion to the Lord and grow in faith?

April 14

Philippians 4:6 "Have no anxiety at all, but in everything, by prayer and petition, with thanksgiving, make your requests known to God."

While Saint Paul wrote this instruction, clearly, it came directly from the Lord. The opposite of trust is fear and anxiety. When anxiety abounds, love becomes very difficult.

What is there to be afraid of? Why not try trusting God? Hasn't He taken care of us throughout our lives? As we turn our lives over to Him in love and trust, His peace fills our souls.

He answers our prayers by blessing us and those we love.

Thank You Lord, for dismissing all anxiety from my mind and for answering my prayers. I praise You for the gift of thanksgiving, and for showing me how to place my trust in You.

What anxieties cause you to cry out for God's help?

Philippians 4:13 "I have the strength for everything through him who empowers me."

This verse definitely should be placed in the very core of our being. It's like a well of living water and should be drawn upon in times of trouble and need.

Often in life, we try to be all things to all people and circumstances. We use our strength and limited wisdom to attempt to solve our problems. We will always fail without God's help. For without Him, we can do nothing.

Lord, help me to realize that the only strength I need is Yours, and without You, I can do nothing. I praise You for your strength and courage in my life.

Do you need to rely more on the Lord to help you in your daily life?

April 16

Luke 7:50 "…'Your faith has saved you; go in peace.'"

In any part of our lives, faith is the only thing that keeps us sane and full of hope for the future. There are times when we all feel like giving up. Sometimes work, a relationship or school just isn't going as planned. Trials and tribulations are common—what do we do?

That is the time we must surrender all to God. Let Him take over family, relationships, businesses, jobs—all our life. Have faith that great things will happen in the future. Then, the peace that passes all understanding will flow into our life like a river of everlasting joy. This river fills our souls with the joy of the Lord.

Lord, increase my faith so that your peace fills my life. I praise You for being the source of my peace.

When are the times you recognize God filling your life with His love and joy? When do you forget that He is part of the joy, strength and peace in your life?

Colossians 3:17 "And whatever you do, in word or in deed, do everything in the name of the Lord Jesus, giving thanks to God the Father through Him."

We make choices each day and we determine how much of the Lord's presence we want in our lives. Do we put Him in a corner and make Him a part-time influence on our behavior? Or, do we want Him front and center in each of our decisions—in everything?

"Everything" means everything, not just what is convenient or inconvenient. What do you want? God will always respect our choices.

Lord, give me the grace to always put you first in every aspect of my day. I praise you for the gift of wisdom.

When do you put God first? When do you not prioritize Him? When do you forget Him completely, out of your own selfishness?

April 18

Matthew 15:11 "It is not what enters one's mouth that defiles that person; but what comes out of the mouth is what defiles one."

It is extremely important that we watch every word we say. We have the power to build or destroy.

In our lives, some people will think what we say is essential. It could be a spouse, child, friend, co-worker or even someone we meet at a party or on the street.

At that moment, find a way of building their confidence. Show how much you love them and how much the Lord loves them by your words and actions.

Thank You, Lord, for giving me the grace to monitor what I say to those around me. Help me to encourage others, and to love them as You love them. I praise You for being the God of encouragement.

When do you fail to encourage others? How can you stop yourself and recognize ways and words to build people up?

Proverbs 12:22 "Lying lips are an abomination to the LORD,/ but those who are truthful are his delight."

Have you ever lied? How did you feel in your spirit and soul? I know, you thought you had a good reason. It was to protect the innocent or some other rationalization that sounded good at the time. However, deep down you knew the truth, but you didn't have the courage to "speak" the truth. Was there a time when you did speak the truth, and you felt the peace of the Lord? You felt His presence and love?

Lord, help me always to speak the truth, no matter the cost. I praise You for being the God of truth, for You are the way, the truth and the life.

When do you feel weak and tell lies or half-truths to those in your life? In your personal life? At work?

Isaiah 55:11 "So shall my word be/ that goes forth from my mouth;/ It shall not return to me void,/ but shall do my will,/ achieving the end for which I sent it."

When God gives us a word on how He will bless us, believe it! When we hear a word from our spouses, friends or co-workers, and we know that word is from the Lord, it will be fulfilled. God's Word is truth—fruit that will be harvested in our lives. The same is true with words that leave our mouths. They will be self-fulfilling prophecies. They will be given power in our lives. Therefore, speak prosperity, health and healing.

Lord, I ask that You bless each word that comes from my mouth today and every day. I praise You for putting Your words in my mind and mouth.

How do you humble yourself to speak only God's words to those around you? Do you praise God for His guidance?

Isaiah 55:9 "As high as the heavens are above the earth,/ so high are my ways above your ways/ and my thoughts above your thoughts."

Often, I think I have to solve my many problems. However, my thoughts, logic and reasoning are limited. But, God's are infinite. My problem may have a million solutions, but God only needs one.

Why not pray and surrender all problems and difficulties to Him? He will bless you beyond your wildest dreams.

Thank You Lord, for loving me and helping me in all aspects of my life. I praise You for blessing my mind with Your love.

Do you let the Lord be a part of your thoughts and glorify Him with your whole being? Do you praise Him for loving you? In prayer, song and actions?

Amos 9:15 "I will plant them upon their own ground;/ never again shall they be plucked/ From the land I have given them,/ say I, the LORD, your God."

God is so generous. No one can ever surpass His generosity. He blesses us and our lives if we ask Him. What is needed? Faith that passes all understanding is essential. Know that if you ask Him for help with your family, job or any of life's obstacles, in time of need, Jesus always delivers. Does that mean that our prayers will be answered exactly the way we want? Perhaps not—but God knows best. He will bless us in the way we need the most.

If we move forward spiritually, and we stay in His will, the ground we have been given will never be taken away. God will plant His blessings in us to our thousandth generation. Praise Him forever!

I praise You Lord for planting blessings with my life and showering me with Your grace.

How do you reflect on the great blessings the Lord has given you?

Genesis 21:22 "...'God is with you in everything you do.'"

An army commander spoke this verse to Abraham. His goodness was clearly seen by all. Is that the same for you?

Recently, I was at an outdoor market buying fruit. I blessed the man selling to me and told him I felt God was blessing his business. He looked at me and told me I had a sign written across my forehead. I looked at him in puzzlement. He said he could always tell a good man because they have a sign written across their forehead broadcasting it. Then, he grasped my hand and blessed me. Wow! I felt God's presence in a powerful way! I was almost knocked over.

Lord, may I today and always have a sign written across my face, witnessing to Your awesome presence in my life. I praise You for being the source of my sign.

Do you pay attention to the people and physical signs that remind you of His love?

Exodus 16:4 "...'I will rain down bread from heaven for you.'

I sometimes fight anxiety over the ups and downs of life. However, God is always consistent. He tells me to stand my ground, to stay firm in my faith and to know that He will bless my activities when they are done in His name. When we trust and praise Him for all things, His blessings flow down from above. Those blessings are like manna from heaven, raining down on us.

I praise You Jesus for all the blessings You rain down on my life and that of my family. Amen.

Can you even recount all your blessings? How do you show your gratitude to the Lord? Do you show gratitude through your actions and prayers?

Deuteronomy 28:2 "When you hearken to the voice of the LORD, your God, all these blessings will come upon you and overwhelm you...."

This is how I feel today. I have asked God to purify my heart—to mold me into His pure vessel. I choose to be holy—to be set apart for my master and Savior. I want only to do His will.

When we surrender in the deepest part of our hearts, God takes over and does the rest; He then speaks, as the saying goes, "early and often." God speaks while we are asleep, upon our waking and all throughout the day. When we listen, His Holy Spirit will come upon us as "tongues of fire."

I praise and thank You Lord, for overwhelming me with Your gracious Love and sending me the Holy Spirit.

How often do you ask the Holy Spirit to enter into your life? Praise God and thank Him for His generosity.

Psalm 23:6 "Only goodness and kindness follow me/ all the days of my life;/ And I shall dwell in the house of the LORD/ for years to come."

Psalm 23 is a very emotional passage for me, especially this verse. A country-western song uses these same words throughout. When I was going through a particularly hard time at my one of my jobs, I would play this song and sing this verse every morning on the way to work.

Recently, at a prayer meeting in our home, a friend gave us a gift. It was a plaque with this same verse. God's love for us is so amazing and hard to even remotely comprehend. We just have to appreciate it!

I praise and thank You Lord for all Your goodness that follows me wherever I go, forever and ever!

Do you feel His presence wherever you go? How do you feel His presence? Do you feel Him in nature and in the eyes and hearts of people you meet?

Psalm 25:21 "Let integrity and uprightness preserve me,/ because I wait for you, O LORD."

It is hard to wait. It is difficult to be patient, especially when we want something badly. It is because we want it so much that God may delay giving us our desire. He wants us to seek Him and nothing else. He is a jealous God who doesn't want competition. What is the reason for this? I believe it is because of His love for us. He wants to make us pure.

Trials and tribulations, the love of money and the lure of worldly things can choke our faith. God is testing us and purifying us. He is creating us in His image.

Lord, may I never sacrifice integrity in the pursuit of success. I praise You for being the source of my integrity.

Do you put other things before God? When do you do this?
How can you always remember to put God first?

April 28

Matthew 21:9 "...blessed is he who comes in the name of the Lord...."

Today is my son's birthday. Praise God for him! God gave me this verse as a prophecy for the birth of our child. We had a girl and a boy and wanted to know what God had in mind for us. This word of knowledge from the Lord almost knocked me off my feet. The baby was to be a boy and be blessed by God. He would receive supernatural favor. I immediately went out and bought a dozen roses for my wife with this verse written on the card.

Guess what? That boy has been a blessing for us and for all who know him. He reflects God's wisdom and talent.

Lord, I praise and thank You for the birth of my son. May You continue to bless him forever!

It is important to remember we are all special to God because we each are His anointed children, created in His image. Do you love people as anointed children of God?

1 Samuel 3:10 "…'Speak, for your servant is listening.'"

An important step in our spiritual journey is hearing, trusting in and opening our heart to God's voice. Is it just my imagination? Am I making it up? Is it my mind, playing tricks on me?

Most spiritual leaders clearly say that without listening to God, we cannot have a relationship with Him. Jesus is living and not dead! He is alive, as we will be alive for all eternity. Through the Holy Spirit, He has not left us orphaned. He is there, guiding and leading us to Him.

Lord, may each of us, each day, say, "Speak, Your servant is listening." I praise You for speaking to me and for telling me how much You love me.

Do you listen to God when you pray fervently to the Lord? When do you praise God for His Love of you?

Luke 1:38 "Mary said, 'Behold, I am the handmaid of the Lord. May it be done to me according to your word.'"

Mary is often seen as an example of Christian humility and values. In this verse, she says no matter what, she wants to do God's will, not her own will. How many of us can say that? Another important aspect of this verse is a reliance on God's Word. When we follow His Word, great things and many blessings are in store for us!

Lord, we submit all that we have in our life to Your Word. Let it be done to us, as You will! I praise You for being the "Word" for us forever.

Do you accept the Lord's Word? Do you trust Him with your whole life? How can you improve in this area of your life?

Luke 1:37 "...for nothing will be impossible for God."

Whatever we do in life, there is a tendency to believe our strength, wisdom and talent make the difference. However, as we know from Scripture, without God, we can do nothing.

In addition, we learn that with God, all things are possible. What are we to do? First, pray for guidance, follow instructions and work as hard as necessary to fulfill God's will in our lives. Rest on the reality that God has infinite ways of blessing us and our lives.

I praise God for making all things possible in my job, family and life.

Do you believe the Lord is needed in your life? When do you trust in Him? When do you fail to do so?

Acts 20:35 "...'It is more blessed to give than to receive.'"

How many of us truly believe this? Then, why don't we give often to those around us? Are we more excited to receive a surprise gift from someone than give one?

The answer tells us quite a bit about ourselves. I do believe that God wants us to be both happy and grateful when we receive a gift. However, when we give, we ask the Lord for the grace to show "agape" love, a love that is unconditional.

Lord, teach me to be a more gracious giver and to love unconditionally. I praise you for your infinite gifts and unconditional love for me.

What gifts and talents do you have to offer others that demonstrate your love for them, thereby sharing the love of Christ?

Hebrews 2:4 "God added his testimony by signs, wonders, various acts of power, and distribution of the gifts of the holy Spirit according to his will."

Jesus wants so much to give us signs, wonders and miracles in our lives. We block them by our unbelief. These gifts were not meant for just a small, select group of people at the time Christ walked on earth. Does that make sense?

It's more logical that a God, who loves us and has not left us orphans, would give us even more gifts. Haven't you done that for those you love? Have faith and receive God's gifts by saying "Yes" to Jesus for taking over your life. Your will is striving to become His will.

Lord, I open my heart to you to take it over. I believe that Your Holy Spirit will overpower me with Your grace when I ask. I praise You for Your blessings.

What do you want to say to the Holy Spirit when you ask Him to enter your heart?

Hebrews 7:25 "Therefore, he is always able to save those who approach God through him, since he lives forever to make intercession for them."

What is love? How is it manifested to us? How does Christ show His love for us? One way, in addition to His death on the cross and saving grace, is His constant intercession for us. However, why should He intercede for us if we don't ask for His help? One could say God already knows what we pray for.

That is true, but Jesus never interferes in our lives unless we ask Him in. Therefore, we must pray without ceasing. We must ask for His help, and He will intercede to the Father on our behalf. Can you think of anything better?

Thank you, Lord, for Your constant intercession for us. I praise Your name for all eternity.

How have you seen God's handiwork in your life? How are you showing gratitude

1 Corinthians 15:57 "But thanks be to God who gives us the victory through our Lord Jesus Christ.

Praise the Lord, now and forever! Think of all the things Jesus has given you through the years.

Write them down. Meditate on them. Praise Him throughout the day.

Jesus is the God of the possible. God makes all things possible when we surrender our lives to Him. If you trust Him, work hard and believe in Him, great things happen.

I praise and thank You Lord for all the wonderful things you are doing and have done for me, my family, friends, ministries and business.

Do you show your thankfulness by praising Him for all that is good in your life?

Psalm 37:7 "Leave it to the LORD,/ and wait for him."

One of the hardest things for all us to do is to be patient. As the song goes, "Wait, wait, on the Lord, for in His time, He makes all things beautiful." But when we wait in the flesh, we worry. We fret. We think we should be doing something. But we are doing the most important thing, because we believe in God's Word and promises. If you are told by the Lord to wait, then wait. However, if you are not to wait, but to act, then act immediately!

Lord, help me to listen to Your voice and Word so I know when to act and when to wait. I praise You for Your voice and love for me.

Do you listen to God when you pray? Are your prayers focused on petition? Do you pray in contemplation and bask in God's loving wisdom? How do you quiet your mind and use your heart to hear His command to act or wait?

James 1:12 "Blessed is the man who perseveres in temptation, for when he has been proved he will receive the crown of life that he promised to those who love him."

Everyone is tempted. Jesus was tempted What defines success in living the Christian life is the amount of love we have for Christ and for each other. When we are full of love, we can overcome temptation. Love ourselves first. When we love ourselves, we are capable of loving others, including God.

Satan wants us to hate ourselves when we fail to resist temptation. Don't! God loves us exactly as we are. He will always help us get through our trials and temptations.

Lord, I praise and thank You for helping me resist my temptations. I love You!

Temptations are everywhere in our daily lives; how do you resist? Prayer and consciously choosing God's will are powerful. Have you used these tools? How can you implement them in times of trial? When could these positive practices have helped in the past?

James 1:22 "Be doers of the word and not hearers only, deluding yourselves."

It is easy to think that our spirituality is going great because we go to church, read the Bible, pray, etc.

However, to put the Word of God into action means that we must be the Word in action. When we surrender to God, He will make sure we love Scripture and put it into action. We will love His people and do everything to help them.

I praise and thank You for giving me the grace to love Your people and live Your Word.

How can you implement more Scripture into your daily life? How in your life can you put what you have learned into action?

May 9

James 3:8 "...but no human being can tame the tongue. It is a restless evil, full of deadly poison."

One second we are praising God, the next, we are cursing or complaining about others around us. The inconsistency can be frustrating to those who sincerely want to follow Jesus. What is the answer?

The answer is to ask God for the fruit of the Holy Spirit—the patience, peace, love and understanding only He can give us.

Lord, I praise and thank You for helping me control my tongue, using it only to glorify Your name and build Your kingdom.

How can you actively work with God to control your tongue and use only words that God wants you to use?

2 Corinthians 12 "...My grace is sufficient for you, for power is made perfect in weakness."

I don't know about you, but I definitely feel powerless most of the time. I know that without God, I can do nothing. And, in my weakness, I realize that only through God can I make a difference in this life.

Pride is the root of all sin. If we had everything together, we wouldn't need God, and we would be full of pride. For example, Lucifer, who was described as the most beautiful angel, put his pride first and then fell.

Thank You, Lord, for giving me the grace to turn my weaknesses into strength. I praise You for teaching me humility.

In what ways has God taught you humility in your life's events? Do you recognize these trials as God's blessings? Do you see Him increasing humility in your life? Do you focus on praising Him with thanks?

2 Peter 1:17 "...'This is my Son, my beloved, with whom I am well pleased.'"

We are the King's kids, His adopted sons and daughters. When we believe, trust, love and are obedient to His Word, we delight Him.

I have often felt God say He was well pleased with me, even when I wasn't pleased with myself. However, Jesus sees through the moment and looks at the heart. He loves us with an everlasting love!

Thank You Lord for loving me with Your eternal love. I praise You for being the God of love.

How do you tell the Lord how much you love Him? Share your words of praise of Him.

1 John 4:16 "We have come to know and to believe in the love God has for us. God is love, and whoever remains in love remains in God and God in him.

God is love and love is all we need. Simply, all life is about understanding how much God loves us and how we respond to that love.

We need to meditate on His love, speak of it and tell others about it. When that happens, our lives become transformed.

We become love in action.

Lord, thank You for teaching me how much You love me and for helping me to love You and others more deeply. Help me to increase all aspects of love in my life. I praise You for being the God of unconditional love.

Do you fully understand God's eternal love? What does it mean to you?

Ephesians 5:20 "...giving thanks always and for everything in the name of our Lord Jesus Christ to God the Father."

In some of my jobs, I have travelled extensively. I remember one particular day. I was struggling to give thanks and praise; my airplane was delayed and an eyelash away from being diverted to another airport 800 miles away.

Then a funny thing happened. I began talking to the gentleman sitting next to me. It turned out he was a strong Christian, an important factor, because we both ended up in prayer and agreed to ask God to stop the severe turbulence. Suddenly, there was a break in the storm, and we landed without a problem. The wind had stopped—just as Jesus had promised when He said <u>we</u> would do as He did and more. I realized, then, why Jesus wants us to give Him thanks in all things. Without the plane's delay, I wouldn't have met my new friend or seen God's blessings in action.

I praise You Jesus and give you thanks for all things!

Do you praise God during difficult times in your life?

Ephesians 6:16 "In all circumstances, hold faith as a shield, to quench all [the] flaming arrows of the evil one."

There may be times when it feels as if the evil one is really trying to make life difficult. Perhaps it is just the flesh or the world. Regardless, it is painful. Yet, I also feel joy as I hold onto God's promises and feel His peace.

I realize faith is essential in this struggle. Only faith will turn the enemy away. It is our shield against the world and evil one. The Lord is here to protect us at all times. Call on Him, because He has not left us defenseless!

Lord, thank you for protecting me against all evil. I praise you for being my protector.

When do you feel you need protection in your life? In personal situations? Work-related?

Isaiah 37:36 "The angel of the LORD went forth and struck down one hundred and eighty-five thousand in the Assyrian camp."

"Know that I am God," says the Lord. "Know that I love you with an everlasting love and that I will always protect you." This is what I hear from God. Many times, I feel God's presence, but I soon begin to feel alone. God wants us to trust in Him and to always know that He holds us in the palm of His hand. The Israelites were in trouble, but God knew that no harm would come to His chosen people. This is true for us, too. When we are with the Lord, no harm will come to us—as long as we trust in Him.

Lord, thank You for protecting me from my enemies. I praise You for being my Father in heaven.

How do you rely on God? Do you sometimes forget He is always there for you?

Proverbs 13:20 "Walk with wise men and you will become wise,/ but the companion of fools will do badly."

In our life, one of the most important choices we can make is our friends, business associates or partners.

Our ability to make friends with Godly, spirit-filled men and women is critical to our spirituality. Whether or not we want to accept it, we are greatly influenced by our friends. To think and act as Christ's disciples on earth, we must walk with those who have the wisdom of the Lord.

Also, we shouldn't yoke ourselves with unbelievers in business. It will tempt us to do things in the flesh that we don't want to do. Spend time with those who nourish you spiritually.

Lord, I praise and thank You for leading me to Godly men and women as friends.

How can you avoid people of the flesh and only choose people who are Godly as your friends?

Proverbs 17:17 "He who is a friend is always a friend,/ and a brother is born for the time of stress."

In my career, I have left jobs, been demoted and fired. In all three cases, people who I thought were friends left me quickly. I couldn't believe it at first. I will never forget those individuals who I called my friends a week earlier, who once made sure they gave me flattering speech, but were now walking in a different direction when they saw me.

However, there were some surprises, later. I found I had friends who I didn't think cared for me, who stood by me in my time of misfortune and trial. These people were no longer just "friends," but my brothers and sisters. They are cherished as divine jewels—gifts from the Lord. Indeed, angels from God!

Praise the Lord for providing human angels, especially in times of stress and trial.

Who are the human angels in your life? What is so wonderful about them? Have they stood by you in hard times?

Romans 8:31 "...If God is for us, who can be against us?"

The powerful eighth chapter of Romans is life changing. This verse is one of many to memorize. It alters how we look at the power we give to people or situations. God is our benefactor. He is our protector. He will only allow people to interact with us according to His perfect will. We are His children. We are often paralyzed by the fear of others. How will we be perceived? How will we be judged? Will we be included? Feelings such as these can cause our stress level to rise sharply.

Lord we praise You for always being "for" us and bringing people into our lives who, in the name of Jesus, are also for us.

If He is for us, why do we worry or fear any human interaction or situation? Do you look for Christ in people you meet and with whom you form relationships?

Ephesians 4:23-24 "...be renewed in the spirit of your minds, and put on the new self, created in God's way in righteousness and holiness of truth."

Being in Christ, a believer, a follower of the Lord, means a complete change, a metamorphosis. When we allow Jesus to take over our lives, we die to our sinful nature. We die to our flesh. We then focus on truth in our lives and the truth of our own behavior.

We let the light of Christ reveal our new selves in Jesus.

God's way is not the world's way. It is filled with grace and blessings. Our new self no longer lives in fear and despair, but in love, faith and hope.

Lord, melt me, mold me, renew me, and create me as your disciple. I praise You for molding me in Your image.

Do you allow God to melt and mold your heart for the better? Or do you become stiff and rigid when He approaches your heart?

John 6:27 "Do not work for food that perishes but for the food that endures for eternal life, which the Son of Man will give you."

Our priorities often differ from what God desires for us. How many times are the desires of our heart actually things of the world: money, position, influence or power?

Ignatius of Loyola put it well: "We should seek poverty, not riches, insults and scorn, not honor, and humility, not pride." These priorities are those that reflect the grace of God in us.

Lord, teach me to work and focus only on priorities that build up your kingdom and my treasure in heaven. I praise You for the grace to seek Your will.

When is it most difficult to focus on God and His will? Do you realize your perseverance in building the God's kingdom will be more fulfilling than any treasures on earth?

Philippians 4:9 "Keep on doing what you have learned and received and heard and seen in me. Then the God of peace will be with you."

Persistence is critical to success in our Christian walk. We must never grow weary of doing good things for the Lord.

When we are in the Lord's grace, we live in His peace.

That is our spiritual barometer. If stress, anxiety and worry fill our thoughts, then we know we are outside of God's will. He did not come that we should live a life of despair and worry. Rather, He came so that our life would be abundant, joyful and full of peace.

Lord, help me to "stay the course," so that Your peace can flow gently through me more and more each day. I praise You for being the Prince of all peace and joy.

Do you feel joy and peace in your life? When? What are some things you can do to allow God's peace flow through you?

Luke 15:32 "[N]ow we must celebrate and rejoice, because your brother was dead, and has come to life again; he was lost and has been found."

We have all been called to a great commission, to be used by Jesus to save souls for His kingdom and to spread the gospel of truth, joy and peace. God wants us to reach out and share His eternal love with all His adopted children. Are you up to the task?

One of my brothers was recently called by God to attend our prayer meeting. I believe his name is written in the Book of Life. I also believe God will use him to save souls in our family—those very close to both of us. Indeed, it is God's plan to use each of us in a very unique way. We have been chosen to make a difference. All we have to do is say "Yes."

Today, I also celebrate my oldest brother's birthday and praise God that he is in my life.

Lord, I praise and thank You for using me as You save the souls of your sons and daughters.

How can you help in the commission of saving souls? What can you do to bring more people to Christ?

John 4:53 "...'Your son will live,' and he and his whole household came to believe."

Jesus came to heal us. He heals us first, and most importantly, by saving us from our sins and wretchedness. He also wants to heal us and our families from spiritual, emotional and physical problems.

In this Scripture story, a royal official from Capernaum asked Jesus to heal his son, in the same way we do for our own families. Jesus told him not to worry and to go home. At that point, the whole family was healed of their "real" problem—their lack of faith.

Jesus asks us to trust and call upon Him for healing so that our faith strengthens, and His kingdom prospers. I praise You, Jesus, for being my healer.

What kind of healing do you need to become more faithful? Do you need physical, spiritual or emotional healing? Ask for healing.

2 Timothy 2:7 "Reflect on what I am saying, for the Lord will give you understanding in everything."

Most of us struggle when trying to discern God's will. Rejoice! God has not left us alone, wondering what to do with our lives. He gave us His Holy Spirit to guide us daily.

In some cases, it appears God has little to say in our daily activities. That is common thinking. The truth is far from that. God cares about everything. Have you seen the level of detail in God's creation and in His universe? What makes you think He doesn't care about what you think and do? He does!

Jesus, I praise and thank You for sending Your Holy Spirit, giving me the wisdom to do Your will in all things.

Do you believe the Holy Spirit can give you wisdom? Have you asked for that gift? What kind of changes would that make in your life—to listen and embrace the gift of wisdom?

Psalm 40:9 "'To do your will, O my God, is my delight,/ and your law is within my heart.'"

To do God's will is a delight for all of us. His will is written in His instruction book, the Bible. As we read the Scriptures, His instructions and laws become burned onto our hearts—to be used to build His kingdom.

On this day, one of my sons graduated from Law School. He is a special person whom God is using to build His kingdom. In the same way, God is using my daughter, my other son, and my son-in-law and daughter-in-law to spread His love to His people. I believe God's law is their delight, both in their jobs and in their lives.

Lord, I praise You for giving me Your law, which burns in my heart, to serve You with all things.

Do you have the faith to follow God's law? Do you need to ask Him for more faith to follow His law? Remember, He is always there to help.

Galatians 5:14 "...'You shall love your neighbor as yourself.'"

I have always found this verse interesting. The first and obvious question is, "Who is my neighbor?" I might add that in reality many of us don't even love ourselves very much.

We know our neighbor symbolizes everyone. Now, I would like for us to reflect on one additional thing. Our neighbor may be that one person who drives you crazy. Or perhaps, someone has greatly hurt you and to whom you no longer speak because it is too painful. God is calling you to reach out to them in love, in the same way that you reach out to those you love the most.

God doesn't make junk. He has made you holy and blameless before Him. He loves you with an everlasting love. It is with that love that we are to love our neighbors. Don't reflect on how much we love ourselves, but how much God loves us.

Praise You Jesus for loving me so that I may love others with that same deep and abiding love.

Will you let God transform your heart to love all His people?

Zechariah 4:6 "...Not by an army, nor by might, but by my spirit, says the LORD of hosts.

Most of us often think that if we just had more of something missing—resources, time, etc.— all our problems would disappear—problems of finances, spirituality, family, work or anything else bothering us today.

Jesus wants us to focus on just one thing—Him. Without believing in our Lord and having faith in Him, it is impossible to please God. This faith unlocks the power of the Holy Spirit in our lives. It is mightier than any army ever has been or could be.

Lord; teach me to rely on your Holy Spirit for everything in my life! I praise You for that gift!

How do you let go of everything? How do you trust in the Holy Spirit? The answer is found in your faith and in the understanding of God's great love for you.

Joshua 4:24 "'...in order that all the peoples of the earth may learn that the hand of the LORD is mighty, and that you may fear the LORD, your God, forever.'"

What does the "hand of the Lord" mean? It is the power and presence of God in our lives. God wants to demonstrate to His people His power "on earth as it is in heaven."

He is looking for volunteers. Those of us who say "Yes," allow His Holy Spirit to work miracles in our lives—miracles that demonstrate God's power, love and salvation. Say "Yes" - then wait and watch for the miracles!

I praise and thank You, Lord, for Your hand in my life and for the miracles You perform each day.

How do you acknowledge the daily miracles in your life, those joyful and treasured moments with loved ones? Furthermore, resting in God's abundant love is truly a miracle to be celebrated daily.

Acts 11:21 "The hand of the Lord was with them and a great number who believed turned to the Lord."

A critical aspect of the Lord's hand in our lives is how he uses us as instruments in saving His people from sin and death. The early church attributed God's hand for its members' grace and power. It is God's hand that propels us to speak with boldness. It is God's hand that saves His people from the evil one.

Lord, may Your hand be with me, my family and my loved ones forever and ever! I love and praise Your holy name.

How do you help bring God's people to Him? Do you allow God to use you as His instrument?

Ephesians 3:19 "...to know the love of Christ that surpasses knowledge, so that you may be filled with all the fullness of God."

I have learned that no matter what is happening in my life, good or bad, the only thing that sustains me is the love of Jesus. When I meditate on God's love, I am transformed into His image. He gives me His love, joy, peace and strength. He fills my soul with His goodness and love.

True knowledge understands how much God loves us. I often meditate and reflect on His love for us demonstrated by His dying for our sins and His humility in taking human form. He loves us just the way we are!

Lord, Your love is everlasting and transforming. I praise Your name for loving me!

Do you meditate on God's love for you? Do you fully understand Jesus' suffering and dying on the cross was completed so that your sins would be forgiven?

2 Chronicles 16:9 "The eyes of the LORD roam over the whole earth, to encourage those who are devoted to him wholeheartedly."

We all have times when we feel a bit forsaken and alone. I like to call it a "pity party." Definitely not an activity of the Lord!

Of course, as is often the case, the spiritual truth is the exact opposite. God is always with us, ready to bless and encourage. Our role is to seek His face and presence through prayer.

God is always watching us and waiting to show His love—through His Word, His servants, His beautiful world and anything else He wants to use. When we say "Yes" to His love, Jesus sends His angels and the Holy Spirit to guide and be with us.

I praise and bless You God for watching over me and sending me Your love through the Holy Spirit.

Do you feel God's presence watching you? What do you feel when you meditate on His presence?

June 1

Matthew 6:13 "[D]o not subject us to the final test,/ but deliver us from the evil one."

A reality of being human is that we are all subject to many temptations. These temptations are often large and obvious, but they may be small and subtle. Even if we don't act on the temptation, we often feel dirty and depressed when we believe the lies of the enemy.

Do not fear! Jesus has overcome every temptation by His dying on the cross for all our sins. He has won the battle for us and broke the bonds of sin! While it isn't a sin to feel tempted, we can remove all temptation through the grace of God. By relying on Jesus, we resist temptation and claim deliverance.

Lord, I praise and thank You for resisting the evil one on our behalf.

What helps you through those difficult times? Maybe you find yourself wanting to say something harsh or untrue to justify yourself. Do you turn to God for help? Do you thank Him for His help?

June 2

1 Corinthians 10:13 "No trial has come to you but what is human. God is faithful and will not let you be tried beyond your strength; but with the trial he will provide a way out, so that you will be able to bear it."

This verse is a critical one for all those in battle against the flesh and the evil one. We must resist evil! And, know that God will assist us in getting out of the mess we probably created in the first place. We must stop being self-absorbed in our pain and suffering and, rather, look for God's "way out." Moreover, we are so used to sinning in certain circumstances that we need to resist the "comfort" of sin. We need to let the Holy Spirit create a new wineskin in our lives.

Help me, Lord, to always look to You in my darkest hour and for saving me from myself. I praise You for creating me as a new creation in You, Christ Jesus.

When have you turned to God for His help in the most sorrowful situations? Do you turn to other worldly things to help you?

Acts 4:20 "'It is impossible for us not to speak about what we have seen and heard.'"

God's wonders and miracles are happening all around us as we go about our daily activities. Often, we take them for granted. It might be our spouse, children, job or the beauty of nature. To do God's will means to talk about these wondrous things and to praise His name for His gifts.

I believe that ignoring and failing to give thanks to God for our blessings and gifts is a sin of pride. The sin is in thinking that somehow, we deserve them or even worse, that our power or charm is the reason for them.

It is important to praise His name for all things and to ask Jesus to open our eyes to see the world and our lives as He does.

Lord, give me the grace to speak boldly of all the signs and wonders in my life, in hopes that others may come to know You. I praise You for the gift of boldness.

Do you honor blessings that God has bestowed upon you? When has your pride gotten in the way of praising God for all the gifts and blessings given to you?

Matthew 5:6 "Blessed are they who hunger and thirst for righteousness,/ for they will be satisfied."

This is one of my favorite verses because it summarizes what our optimal attitude should be concerning God. When praying this verse, I picture myself alone in the desert, without food or water. How hard would I look for the food and water required to sustain my life? Without food, I would have no chance to be built up; without water, I would wither and die.

The seeking of sustaining food and water should pale in comparison to how much I should long for Jesus. He is the living water and food that gives everlasting life. We must have for Jesus that same thirst and hunger we have in the desert, and then some.

How do we measure up?

Jesus, may I hunger and thirst for you, so that my soul is filled at all times. I praise you for being the source of my hunger for you.

Do you thirst for the Lord's fulfillment or do you turn to other things to be satisfied? When does this happen in your life? Maybe you seek wealth, material objects or beauty.

Luke 10:19 "Behold, I have given you the power to 'tread upon serpents' and scorpions and upon the full force of the enemy and nothing will harm you."

Let me repeat this: "Nothing will harm you." Nothing? Nothing! God's grace is all-powerful. When the enemy comes against us with its slings and arrows, we rejoice for victory is near. Use faith as a shield and the Word of God as a sword. Speak God's promises, using His Word! Use all the weapons at your disposal and praise the name of Jesus. Then, the enemy will flee before you.

Victory is yours.

Lord, I praise and thank You for protecting me against the enemy and keeping me from harm.

Do you recognize the enemy attacking you? Do you seek the Lord for protection or do you rely on things of this world? Do you praise God for His help or do you only see the struggles you face?

Micah 6:8 "You have been told, O man, what is good,/ and what the LORD requires of you:/ Only to do the right and to love goodness,/ and to walk humbly with your God."

There are so many things in our lives that feel so complicated. What to do about our job? Should I marry that person? Have children? How should I serve God?

God wants to simplify our lives. He tells us, through the prophet Micah, to do right. We know in our heart what is right and wrong. We don't need someone to tell us. It is written in our heart.

To love goodness is to devote our life to following God's law and ways. In doing so, we naturally walk humbly before the Lord. And, we soon realize goodness occurs only through God's grace.

Lord, teach me to love only You—the center of my life— so that I may do right, seek goodness and walk humbly before You. I praise You for Your guidance.

How do you make God the center of your life? In what ways can you improve upon this relationship? Do you ask God for the guidance to follow Him? Do you read the Scriptures for guidance?

Exodus 20:12 "Honor your father and your mother, that you may have a long life in the land which the Lord, your God, is giving you."

Most of us quickly recognize this verse. Yes, it states that we should honor our father and mother. However, my guess is that most of us do not know the blessing that accompanies this command. God will honor us abundantly by the love we show our parents. He will bless us with a long, and I believe, fruitful life.

With the demanding lives most of us have, we might think it a burden to see or even keep in touch with our parents. If that is the case, we must question our priorities! If we won't even take time to be with our parents, then how much time will we give to God? They usually go together.

Lord, help me to love Your commandment to honor my father and mother. Because I seek to honor You, may I love them as You love them. I praise You for giving me the gift of parents and those who have taken care of me in the past and present.

Do you appreciate your parents for their love and guidance? Maybe your parents are no longer alive. Do you reflect on the relationship you had?

1 Corinthians 2:15-16 "The spiritual person, however, can judge everything but is not subject to judgment by anyone. For 'who has known the mind of the Lord, so as to counsel him?' But we have the mind of Christ."

The closer I get to the Lord, the more I realize how I think differently than most people in the world. I see world events or other activities that affect my life in a more spiritual context, not that of the flesh. I strongly believe that as we surrender to God, we take on His mind. In so doing, He gives us wisdom to make the right decisions.

Furthermore, He asks us not to "yoke" ourselves with nonbelievers. By doing so, we will be in constant turmoil because they think in the flesh and we discern in the spirit of God.

I praise and thank You Lord, for giving me the mind of Christ and for helping me make better decisions that reflect Your will.

Do you guard yourself from the influence of nonbelievers; are you mindful of God's will for you?

John 16:33 "'I have told you this so that you might have peace in me. In the world you will have trouble, but take courage, I have conquered the world.'"

As the saying goes, "I never promised you a rose garden."

But even if we do get a rose garden, it is filled with thorns as well as beautiful flowers.

Yes, there will be trouble in our lives. Rejoice! For Jesus has overcome them all. He has filled you with His Holy Spirit. He has conquered the enemy. For Him, nothing is impossible. Why do you still doubt? Has He not taken care of your life up to this point? When you've trusted Him, hasn't He made all things turn into blessings? I know Jesus has done so in my life!

Thank You, Lord, for conquering everything I will face today and tomorrow, just as You did yesterday. I praise the name of Jesus!

Do you appreciate and praise Jesus for conquering the grave and dying for your sins? What does that mean to you?

Psalm 51:4 "Thoroughly wash me from my guilt/ and of my sin cleanse me."

Trials and tribulations—they happen to all of us. Rather than trusting God fully and completely, one can easily fall into a life of the flesh, leading to doubt, depression and despair. My own lack of trust in the Lord was revealed to me by God to be my biggest sin. This lack of trust opened the door for other behaviors that fell outside of God's will. It was the sin of pride. My trouble was bigger than God's solution, I thought, so I had to try to solve it myself.

I know God's love is unwavering. I may move away from Him but His love for me will never change. When I turn to Him, He washes me whiter than snow. He cleanses me and removes my guilt. Indeed, that is why He died for me.

Lord, You are faithful even when I am not. Increase my faith, so that I may love You without ceasing! I praise You for being the God of mercy.

God is perfect, and often we struggle to be faithful to His perfect will. What things need to change in your heart? Do you need a transformation of the heart? Ask Him to aid you in this!

1 John 1:9 "If we acknowledge our sins, he is faithful and just and will forgive our sins and cleanse us from every wrongdoing."

To sin is part of the human condition. We die so that we can live permanently in the state of grace with the Lord. When we sin, we separate ourselves from God's will in our lives. However, He never leaves us and remains forever faithful. He waits only for us to "acknowledge His mercy, forgiveness and grace. Then God cleanses us, as if our sin never happened.

Lord, I praise and thank You for being my Savior and healer.

How do you ask the Lord to help you examine your sins? Look deep in your heart to find your burdens and give them to God.

Genesis 22:12 "...'I know now how devoted you are to God, since you did not withhold from me your own beloved son.'"

How much do you love God? Would you give up anything for Him? Abraham was asked to give his only son, a most cherished and beloved part of his life. He said "Yes" to God.

The response from God is always the same. Blessings!

When we die to what is important to us, God takes over our lives. And, because we put Him first, the fruits of the Holy Spirit, joy, peace and love, take over.

I pray that I put You first, Lord, before anything else in my life. I praise You for Your everlasting love.

What are you willing to give up for the Lord? Are you ready to commit your whole life, your marriage, your family members, your work and your daily life? Are you ready to offer it up to God as your sacrifice? Now, think about how God offered up His Son, Jesus Christ. Reflect! Ask the Lord to help you examine your sins.

1 John 2:15 "Do not love the world or things of the world. If anyone loves the world, the love of the Father is not in him."

This verse is difficult for those who want to keep one foot in the world and one foot with God. The reality is that God wants all of us, not just the part we want to give Him. He is a jealous God who doesn't like competition.

When we love the things of the world, we begin to lust after them and worship them as idols. We create a god for ourselves, similar to the golden calf the Israelites built in the desert. This idol worship must be eradicated from our body, soul and spirit.

Lord, melt me, mold me and transform me into Your image. Help me to love only You and not the pleasures of the world. I praise You in all things!

Are you ready to take your whole life and surrender it to Christ? What are the challenges in this world that hold you back? Is it worthwhile to you to let God transform your life? Ask the Lord to help you examine your sins. Look deep in your heart to find your burdens and give them to God.

Romans 8:32 "He who did not spare his own Son but handed him over for us all, how will he not also give us everything else with him?"

No one can ever exceed God's generosity, kindness, love and gentleness. He supplies our every need, in accordance with His riches and glory.

Jesus, who loves us beyond our comprehension, wants to shower us with gifts: the fruits of the Holy Spirit. They are His everlasting blessings.

Lord, I praise and thank You for blessing me by fulfilling all my needs.

Count your blessings from the Lord. What needs does He fulfill in your life?

Revelation 2:10 "Do not be afraid of anything that you are going to suffer...Remain faithful until death, and I will give you the crown of life."

In this world, there will be suffering. We know this and usually try to avoid it. The question is, "How do we respond to adversity?" I believe we need to embrace suffering in the way that Jesus did—"Thy will be done in our lives."

Jesus will always bear our burdens and give us the strength to endure. When we finish the race, we will receive the eternal crown of life.

I praise You Jesus for helping me through my suffering, as I wait patiently for the crown of life.

Jesus has put Himself in your shoes all the days of your life. He empathizes with your suffering and bears your crosses with you. Are you patient and ready to praise God for your suffering? And do you trust in what He is doing in your life?

June 16

Song of Songs 3:4 "...I took hold of him and would not let him go...."

On this date, one particular Father's Day, my wife gave me an incredible card with this Scripture verse written in it. I feel so blessed to have a wonderful wife who is both filled with the Holy Spirit and the mother of our children. I am blessed to be the father of three fantastic children, whom I am very proud.

My wife of more than 45 years and my children are not letting me go. How much more so is Jesus not abandoning me? Like a faithful spouse, God will always be at our side.

I praise and thank You Lord for blessing me with a wonderful family and allowing me to be a father to Your children.

What do you love most about your family? Praise God!

1 Peter 4:8 "Above all, let your love for one another be intense, because love covers a multitude of sins."

Our flesh is weak, and mistakes will happen in our lives. Obviously, it is important to repent and strive to never sin again. Strive to be perfect, as the Lord is perfect. Unfortunately, most of us are "works in progress." We often repeat our weaknesses. What to do? Peter has one suggestion: love. We need to love one another and the Lord with all our might. Indeed, love will cover a multitude of our weaknesses. In fact, in St. Paul's writings, we learn that in weakness we are strong. I believe it is then—in our weaknesses—that we rely solely on the Lord.

Today I celebrate the birthday of two wonderful people who are full of love: my mother, who is heaven praying for me, and my daughter-in-law.

Lord, I praise You for helping me to passionately love You, my family members and my neighbors.

It isn't always easy to love family members, neighbors, co-workers and friends. What do you need from God to help you find the good in others? We need to love them because God loves them, and He wants you to love them too!

1 Peter 2:24 "He himself bore our sins in his body upon the cross, so that, free from sin, we might live for righteousness. By his wounds you have been healed."

This verse says it all. It was our sins that led Jesus to die on the cross. It was our pride, our stubbornness and our rebellious nature. We have eternity to thank our Lord and Savior for redeeming us.

Through Jesus dying on the cross, we now can be "right" with God. This "becoming right" enables us to live according to His will. And, it puts us in the state of grace, allowing us to be "righteous" before God.

We are healed because of the cross. The wounds Jesus suffered for us are symbolic of our sin, and because our sins are healed, we are healed.

I praise You, Jesus, for being the God of healing.

What has God already healed in your life? With what healing do you need His help?

John 21:17 "'Do you love me?'...'Feed my sheep.'"

Jesus asks each of us today if we love Him. Do we answer "Yes" without thinking? That is what Peter did. Jesus had to ask him three times, each time with a deeper request for unconditional love. Love with a love that is not self-serving, conditional or occasional, but a love unwavering and passionate. It must be a love that focuses on serving others.

When Jesus said "Feed My sheep," He was obviously referring to us. We are to feed each other spiritually, emotionally and physically.

Lord, I praise You for helping me to love as You love. Give me the grace to reach out to Your sheep and love in Your name.

Do you sometimes lack love for all God's sheep? Why is it so difficult to love all His people, knowing full well that God loves you unconditionally? Is it part of being human?

Psalm 34:7 "When the afflicted man called out, the LORD heard,/ and from all his distress he saved him."

Some days are very difficult for all of us. Our troubles mount; things don't go right; then we get depressed. What do we do in these moments? Do we give up and give in to such sinful behaviors as anger, drinking or immorality, etc.?

Jesus has the solution for us. He is there to take our burdens. He comforts us and helps us to see the bigger picture. He only asks one thing: that we turn to Him and ask Him to come into our lives. By our humility, we will be redeemed.

Lord, I praise and thank You for taking on my distress and assisting me in all things.

Are you like the blind man and believe even during the most sorrowful or frustrating times?

Leviticus 19:18 "Taken no revenge and cherish no grudge against your fellow countrymen. You shall love your neighbor as yourself."

In life, some people, for one reason or another, do not support us. We get upset, for example, when we learn they are spreading rumors or insults about us. If we are of the world, we may think about retribution or revenge.

However, we are not of the world. As Christians, we know God's ways are not our own. We are not to seek revenge, but to love our enemies—even when they hurt us beyond what we think we can endure. We are to pray daily and cherish those who turn against us.

Lord, I praise and thank You for helping me to seek Your face and Your wisdom in my dealings with others.

How does it benefit you to see the Lord in the people you spend time with?

Deuteronomy 30:6 "The LORD, your God, will circumcise your hearts and the hearts of your descendants, that you may love the LORD, your God, with all your heart and all your soul, and so may live."

What does it mean to "circumcise your heart"? This promise, I believe, relates to a covenant with God regarding circumcision. It means that when we are obedient to God's Word and calling, our hearts will become one with His.

In looking at the big picture of God's love for us, if we choose to follow Him, He will bless us and our descendants down to the 100th generation. This is both a great responsibility and a great blessing.

I praise and thank You Lord for the circumcision of my heart and that of my family so that I may love You with all my heart, soul and mind forever!

How has God purified your heart so that you can love Him fully?

Acts 28:5 "But he shook the snake off into the fire and suffered no harm."

The Lord is good. He will protect us from all evil. He will surround us with His angels and goodness. We need not fear anything from man, the world or the devil.

Paul, in this story, shows us that even a poisonous snake can do us no harm when we are in the will of the Lord. I believe this snake represents any evil that attacks us. God will protect us and keep us safe.

I praise and thank You, Lord, for protecting us from all evil with the shield of Your love, grace and joy.

How has God protected you from harm in your life? You have so much to thank Him for.

Proverbs 4:25 "Let your eyes look straight ahead/ and your glance be directly forward."

One of the most challenging, yet essential, element to our spiritual growth is to see clearly the reality of God's will in our lives. I know sin blocks spiritual vision. When we have sinned, it is critical that we sincerely repent immediately. It is only then that we see the spiritual truths that surround us.

Another deterrent to spiritual vision and wisdom is lack of faith. If we believe it is impossible to see the truth of God's message for us, we never will. As the Scripture says, it is impossible to please God without faith.

Only after the men on the road to Emmaus broke bread with Jesus were their eyes were opened. Perhaps that has also happened to you? By being trapped by the world, we have been blinded from God's truth.

Help me, O Lord, to open my eyes to Your truth. May I always look forward and not behind. I praise You for Your mercy.

In what areas of your life do you need the Lord's help? What do you need to see more clearly God's presence in your life?

Matthew 20: 30-34 "Two blind men...cried out, '[Lord,] Son of David, have pity on us!' The crowd warned them to be silent, but they called out all the more...Jesus stopped and called them and said, 'What do you want me to do for you?' They answered him; 'Lord, let our eyes be opened.' Moved with pity, Jesus touched their eyes. Immediately they received their sight, and followed him."

This story personifies many key elements of the Christian walk: reaching out to others, healing the sick, preserving faith and praising God. The blind men did not give up when told to be silent.

How often does our weak faith falter under trial or persecution? Do we ask to be healed? Do we want to be used by the Lord to heal others? Do we persevere when the Lord asks us to be patient? When we are healed, it is critical to praise God, tell others and follow in His footsteps to receive greater miracles and grace.

Lord, open my eyes and heal my blindness so that I may be used by You to build the kingdom. I praise You for being my healer.

What blinds you? What prevents you from seeing how God works in your life? What must you do to receive His healing?

Matthew 20:16 "[T]he last will be first, and the first will be last."

This may be a difficult verse for those who have grown up in a capitalist society, a part of the American culture. Indeed, the parable of the laborers is told to us for a very specific reason. We learn, even more, that God's ways are not the ways of the world, and His mercy is far different from what we experience in our daily lives. In God's eyes, we are all unworthy of His grace. Therefore, we are to share in it equally—our sins are equally forgiven. When Jesus died on the cross, He washed us all whiter than snow, and equally, we receive His grace.

Thank You Lord for saving me, no matter at what point of my life I am. I praise You for being my redeemer and my Savior.

When you fully surrender to God, you are saved by His unconditional love. Reflect on His amazing love.

Luke 14:33 "In the same way, every one of you who does not renounce all his possessions cannot be my disciple."

A major life lesson for me was the realization that a job, career or anything else must not become a "god" in my life. Unfortunately, it can happen without our realizing it. A test for this is observing the stress and anxiety that occurs when things don't go the way we think they should. If we have the proper perspective, the only thing that should be important is our serving and praising God.

God is not interested in our success in life, but in our faithfulness. When we are faithful, He will bless us beyond our comprehension. No one can even come close to God's generosity.

Lord, thank You for teaching me that the only thing important is serving You. I praise You for Your grace.

Do you reflect on the Lord's amazing love? His grace in your life?

Proverbs 18:10 "The name of the LORD is a strong tower;/ the just man runs to it and is safe."

The only thing that will sustain us through life's difficulties is the Lord. Why do we constantly try other methods such as material things, pride, power or illicit sexual relationships? They are cheap copies of God's grace and never satisfy longer than the moment. The way of the Lord lasts for an eternity.

Have you known someone who relies on their wealth for their security? Perhaps it is a 401K or the stock market, etc. I once thought it was in my stock options until the company's value decreased by 70%! I realized then my security lies only in the Lord. That is a lesson that I praise God for!

Lord, You are my tower and strength. May I rely only on You for my present and future. I praise You for Your blessings.

The biggest investment you can make in your life is working on your relationship with God. How much have you invested?

Psalm 116:17 "To you will I offer sacrifice of thanksgiving,/ and I will call upon the name of the LORD."

As we strive for holiness, we are brought to the threshold of praise. What is praise? When do we praise?

I believe praise is communion with God. That is because the Trinity is in constant praise with each other.

Scripture tells us that we were created for praise. Our sacrifice is to die to our own will and adopt God's will, thus choosing to die to our own desires. By doing so, we enter His throne of grace and receive His peace.

May my life be a sacrifice of praise for all of eternity. Lord, teach me to praise You in all things and at all times.

Is it easy for you to keep your focus on God and sacrifice worldly things? What helps you to focus on God—prayer, daily mass, the Rosary?

John 10: 11 "I am the good shepherd. A good shepherd lays down his life for the sheep."

As a leader or someone who strives to be an excellent employee, it is critical that we put first those we work for or with.

The work place can be very competitive, and we often want to be first or demand others to "get out of my way."

However, we know God's way is not our way. We must direct our attitude toward humility and trust in putting Jesus before all else. In this way, we can all be good shepherds to those we encounter.

Come, Lord Jesus, help me lead and guide Your sheep and light the path of Your flock. I praise You for being my Good Shepherd.

Do you give up your personal desires to follow the Lord? What have you given up to follow Him?

July 1

Psalm 108:2 "My heart is steadfast, of God; my heart is steadfast;/ I will sing and chant praise."

To have a steadfast heart is to have an unwavering heart. That means we can't be "in the world" one day, dealing with carnal thoughts and desires, and then try to be a Christian for a few hours on Sunday.

For most of us, a lack of being connected to Jesus "24/7" is a major weakness in our spiritual growth. To grow stronger, we must praise His name, even when we don't feel like it. We must be with Him through thick and thin, mirror His gracious and loving heart, love our neighbors as ourselves and love God with all our heart, soul and might. Furthermore, we must listen to the Word of God, so that we may grow in holiness.

Jesus, may Your praise be ever at my lips.

In all instances of your life, do you praise God? How do you find ways to praise Him at all times?

July 2

1 Corinthians 9: 25 "Every athlete exercises discipline in every way. They do it to win a perishable crown, but we an imperishable one."

Saint Paul wants us to know that we should not focus on the race for success in this world; rather, we should seek the crown of life at the finish line.

What is the percentage of time for our stay here on earth versus eternity? Close to zero. Yet, despite that, we worry, fret and complain about the events of our lives.

I praise You, Lord, for giving me the imperishable crown of life.

Are you living for the hope of eternal salvation or are you only able to see the rewards of this world?

Psalm 41:2 "Happy is he who has regard for the lowly and the poor;/ in the day of misfortune the LORD will deliver him."

Life has its ups and downs. A depiction of godly character is can be found in the way an individual handles adversity. For ourselves, do we give up our spiritual principles or do we draw even closer to the Lord? God gives us a hint on how to handle this. He tells us that we need to take care of the less fortunate. In this way, blessings will flow to them and back to us. Also, by focusing on "lowly and the poor," we forget our own problems.

Lord, give me a heart of charity and goodness. I praise You for all the gifts You have given me.

Do you feel joy in being charitable? Do you see that joy as a gift that comes from God?

Deuteronomy 28:1 "'...if you continue to heed the voice of the LORD, your God, and are careful to observe all his commandments which I enjoin on you today, the LORD, your God, will raise you high above all the nations of the earth.'"

On this July 4th, it is important to reflect on the culture of our country, the United States of America. I believe we are blessed because our nation was founded on Christian values. I feel strongly, that if we live those principles today, it will continue to be blessed. Sometimes, living in this great country of wealth and prosperity, it can be difficult, as a nation, to humble ourselves and praise God for the blessings He has given our country!

God bless America and keep us safe. Help us to follow Your will. We praise You for all Your blessings.

Reflect on how you are sharing the good news of Jesus Christ with your countrymen. Do you pray and give thanks for the blessings bestowed on our country?

2 Corinthians 4:8 "We are afflicted in every way, but not constrained; perplexed, but not driven to despair."

If you have ever tried to start anything new, like a new company or job, you can relate to this verse. There are times when it seems very little goes right. Indeed, those times can be very disturbing and perplexing.

The answers you may be searching for can be found in faith, that is, faith to believe that Jesus is right there with you, your family, and your job. And, by following Him and obeying His Word, you will be blessed.

Lord, give me the grace to have faith in my future and in every circumstance, whether good or bad. I praise You for the gift of faith.

Do you feel God's gift of faith when confronting new challenges in life? Do you acknowledge Jesus is always there, supporting, guiding and loving you?

Psalm 27:14 "Wait for the LORD with courage; be stouthearted, and wait for the LORD."

I love Psalm 27 for so many reasons—especially this verse. We often hear the necessity of waiting on the Lord. The big difference for me is the focus on the word "courage."

Indeed, it takes courage to wait on the Lord, as well as much patience. We all know it is not easy to wait. It is human nature for most of us to want what we want, when we want it. Of course, that impatience is what children desire. As we grow in our faith, our patience should follow.

As I learn more about sin, it is evident, that sin and instant gratification go together. When I am in pain, my flesh wants to respond with addictive behaviors, materialism, power, anger, pride—all of which lead to anxiety and depression.

Lord, give me the courage to wait on Your timing. I praise You for being a God of patience.

Patience in the Lord's plan is faith that trusts in God. How do you deal with God timing?

Matthew 17:20 ""...if you have faith, the size of a mustard seed, you will say to this mountain, "Move from here to there," and it will move. Nothing will be impossible for you.""

Have you ever seen a mustard seed? It is so small you can barely see it. Yet, the same small amount of faith is all we need to find miracles in our lives.

In our culture, it is hard for us to relate to this verse. It seems like make-believe. Yet, Jesus was clearly making the point that faith will change our world in a profound way. It is faith that builds "kingdoms on earth as in heaven."

I praise and thank You, Lord, for building my faith through Your grace. I pray that I have the faith of a mustard seed.

Do you want your faith to grow like a mustard seed? You just need a little faith and God will let it grow into a faith of epic proportions. What would that mean to you? Do you believe? You must take that step of faith for God to act in your life!

Isaiah 43:1 "Fear not, for I have redeemed you;/ I have called you by name: you are mine."

Maybe things aren't going well for you today. Perhaps you are a little blue or depressed.

The antidote is praying and meditating on this Scripture.

Allow the words to permeate your spirit. It is obvious that with God on our side, we have nothing to fear. Ever! We have been freed from the chains and slavery of sin. God knows each of us intimately—He knows each of us by name. and has for all of eternity. We are His children, and He will always protect and defend us.

Lord, I praise Your name for Your redemption, for calling me by name and for being my Father.

Do you rely on the Father to guide you in times of confusion, sadness or grief?

Isaiah 40:29 "He gives strength to the fainting;/ for the weak he makes vigor abound."

I don't know about you, but there are days when I don't feel like getting out of bed. Perhaps I am tired from travel, working too many hours or just exhausted from today's frantic pace. In the darkest days, I don't want to face what I think might happen.

When I turn to Jesus during those moments, I feel His presence. He tells me that I am not alone. I am told not to worry because God will give me His strength to get through the day. He is the Creator who has not abandoned His people.

Lord, I call upon You today and every day to fill my heart with Your presence and to give me Your strength. I praise You for Your love.

Do you ask Our Father to enter your heart? Does feeling His presence bring you joy and love?

July 10

Isaiah 1:18 "Come now, let us set things right,/ says the LORD:/ Though your sins be like scarlet,/ they may become white as snow...."

Shame is a terrible thing. Guilt can be beneficial if it leads us to the Holy Spirit and becomes a catalyst for repentance. Unfortunately, the enemy uses shame as a vehicle to defeat us and immobilize our Christian walk. We stop evangelizing and ministering to others because the accuser wants us to focus on our sins and unworthy feelings.

The reality is we are all sinners and thus unworthy of receiving grace. However, Jesus sacrifice—His death on the cross—makes us worthy through His blood and redemption. Jesus is our defender before the throne of the Father in heaven.

If Satan tries to remind us of our past, remind him of his future!

Lord, I praise and thank You for washing me clean. Help me to always reflect on your mercy and to let my light shine for others.

Do you defend your joy and love from the Lord by praising God the Father? If you rely on the Father and put Him above all things, your joy cannot be taken from you!

Isaiah 54:15 "Should there be any attack, it shall not be of my making;/ whoever attacks you shall fall before you."

From the time we were very small, we have all experienced attacks from others. The root cause might have been gossip, jealousy, pride, revenge or a host of other reasons.

Regardless, it doesn't matter, because the only important thing is that God protects His people. Attacks will bounce off you harmlessly. Also, by attacking you, your attackers will sow what they reaped.

Lord, bless Your holy name, and I praise You for Your protection —and for being my God.

Do you let attacks affect you? Do you ignore them, remain silent and let them pass? Do you pray for the person attacking you? Reflect on the power of such prayer.

John 7:38 "Whoever believes in me, as scripture says:/ 'Rivers of living waters will flow from within him.'"

As you may recall, when Jesus was dying on the cross, a soldier thrust his lance into Jesus' side and both blood and water flowed out. I believe this phenomenon was symbolic of the living water of Jesus!

What does it mean to have living water? We know water is the majority constituent of our bodies. When we accept Jesus as our Savior, we overcome the final curse—death. While our bodies will eventually die, our souls, like a river, will flow forever in the light of Jesus.

Jesus, bless me and transform me into living eternal water so that I may live with You forever! I praise You for being the God of transformation.

Are you open to transformation? What do you need transformed? Forgiveness? Depression? Addiction?

1 John 3:18 "Children, let us love not in word or speech but in deed and truth."

I am sure you may have heard the adages that "talk is cheap" or that we must "walk the walk." These sayings are probably related to this verse from John's epistle. John, as is his style, usually writes in the extreme. If we are to be holy, we must give God all that we have. I have often thought about the comment that if anyone followed us around today to convict us of the crime of being a Christian, would they find any evidence? Or are we so private in our faith that no one ever knows our convictions? Nothing was timid about Jesus. Everyone knew where He stood.

Jesus, give us the boldness to reveal our convictions every day. I praise You for the gift of boldness.

If you act in boldness you are being courageous? How do you stand up for your faith? Do you evangelize by sharing your faith?

1 Peter 3:17 "For it is better to suffer for doing good, if that be the will of God, than for doing evil.

There are times in our lives when we suffer. I believe many times suffering happens because of our own sinfulness and rebellion. However, at other times, it is due to attacks from the world or the evil one.

God allows suffering to happen so we may grow in faith and rely on Him. For God disciplines His children and has not left them orphans.

Lord, lead me, melt me and mold me in the way best for my spiritual growth. I praise You for the gift of the Holy Spirit.

Are you open to change? Are you open to giving the Father your whole life, breaking you down and rebuilding you in His image? Do you welcome the Holy Spirit?

2 Corinthians 4:18 "...as we look not to what is seen, but what is unseen; for what is seen is transitory, but what is unseen is eternal."

Where is our focus? Do we focus on the things of this world, which pass away? Or are we building eternal treasure in heaven?

It is very easy to get trapped by what we see, taste and feel. To devote our energy and actions toward the material leads us down the path of lusting after what the world gives. It will never bring us peace or the fruits of the Holy Spirit. Indeed, our focus must be on loving God and our neighbors and building God's kingdom on earth.

Lord, change my heart to center on Your heavenly treasure. I praise You for the grace of building God's kingdom on earth.

Do you focus on the fruits of this world or the treasures of heaven? Is it hard to conceptualize the greatest treasure? Imagine having everlasting life in heaven with God? What will it be like?

Daniel 3:85 "Servants of the Lord, bless the Lord;/ praise and exalt him above all forever."

When we praise God, we share in His glory. It is essential to understand that God wants us to praise Him at all times. That is difficult, because we usually confuse praise with thanksgiving—and we only do that when things are great. It is essential to praise Him even when we don't feel like it, and even when we are disappointed in life's events.

We praise God for our benefit, not because God is trying to be selfish. He wants His glory and blessings to be with us at all times. When we praise Him, His grace flows through us, and we shine like a bright light.

Jesus, I praise and exalt Your blessed name! I love You!

Are you praising God right now? This very moment you should praise Him for what He is doing in your life! Reflect on the type of commitment God is asking of you.

1 Kings 5:9 "...God gave Solomon wisdom and exceptional understanding and knowledge, as vast as the sand on the seashore.

When asked what grace he wanted from God, I believe Solomon answered astutely when he requested wisdom. With wisdom, our eyes are opened to see the will of God and how He wishes to use us for the good of His kingdom and for the good of others.

It is important to ask for wisdom on a daily basis. What makes wisdom difficult to maintain is sin in our lives. As you recall, it was sin that eventually cost Solomon achievement of his spiritual goals.

Lord, we praise and thank You for the grace of wisdom to serve Your people according to Your will.

Do you want the gift of wisdom? What would that mean for you? How would God's gift of wisdom transform your life?

Proverbs 9:10 "The beginning of wisdom is the fear of the LORD,/ and knowledge of the Holy One is understanding."

Few of us dwell on the concept of "fearing God." Maybe the idea is just too negative. To fear something is considered negative and to be avoided.

But fearing God is completely different. Fear of God is understanding who God truly is and the nature of His relationship with us. God is not our equal nor someone who can be deceived. He is the Almighty who has been and ever will be. He is all-knowing, all-powerful and all-loving.

It is critical that we never fear anything on earth or any man—that we only fear being separated from our God, our Creator.

Lord, help me to fear You so that my wisdom will grow. I praise You for the gift of "fear of the Lord."

When you put the Lord first in your life, you become a God-fearing disciple. When you fear Him, you are blessed. Can you imagine the Lord not in your life? That thought should build up your faith and impel you to hold on dearly to your God!

Romans 12:12 "Rejoice in hope, endure in affliction, persevere in prayer."

Faith and hope are intertwined. If we believe God will take care of our needs and bear our burdens, we hold the seeds of hope. As we hope, we must rejoice in the fact that we have the grace to hope, which helps us to avoid depression or the urge to give up. In fact, I believe that the devil only wins if we give up and stop trying. When affliction occurs, we can endure by utilizing prayer. Only through prayer are we able to get through the difficult times. Once again, hope then takes over. When this reality takes root, God's blessings and grace flow into your life.

Lord, teach me to always hope, even in my afflictions, and to pray without ceasing. I praise You for the gift of prayer.

Do you look to prayer in times of need or despair? How do you feel when you come out of prayer? Do you feel comfort and joy in the Lord?

Romans 10:9 "[F]or, if you confess with your mouth that Jesus is Lord and believe in your heart that God raised him from the dead, you will be saved."

There is nothing complicated about being a Christian. It is about faith and being transformed by that same faith. In that way, our works reflect our new creation in Christ.

To begin the process, we need to confess our convictions openly and publicly. It is not enough to believe in Jesus. We must see Him as our Savior and Redeemer. For even the devil believes that He is God. By trusting Him, you will receive everlasting salvation.

Lord, I believe You are my Lord and Savior. I praise and thank You for Your saving grace!

Do you speak of your faith with conviction? Do you share your faith? That is how you evangelize and receive great blessings! What would help you to evangelize? Do you need to ask for the gift of courage?

Romans 10:15 "…'How beautiful are the feet of those who bring [the] good news!'"

When I reflect on my purpose in life, I often think of this verse, as you may as well. I believe God wants us to be hope for the world so that we all may be united in the next.

It is not about cars, jobs, titles, material things, power or the best of anything. Our purpose is about love, hope and faith. It is about understanding that we have a God who has always—and will always—love us.

People who you encounter today are anxious to hear this Good News. They probably don't even know it. Indeed, you have God's beautiful feet and soul when you proclaim the Good News.

Lord, I thank You for allowing me to be the messenger of Your saving and wonderful news!

Take a look at your feet. Your feet are to serve God. Ask God what He wants you to do, so that you may be a messenger of His living Word. How are you a messenger of God's Word?

Genesis 3:8 "When they heard the sound of the LORD God moving about in the garden at the breezy time of the day, the man and his wife hid themselves from the LORD God among the trees of the garden."

We were created to live in God's presence. The sin of Adam and Eve, thus our sin, caused our separation from Him. Our entire existence on earth is an attempt to reconnect with God's presence. I believe that we do this through praise and worship, our sacrifices and obedience. However, God desires not our sacrifices, but our faith. Therefore, by praising Him for all things, we trust Him and, thus, enter into His holy chambers and presence.

Adam and Eve stopped trusting God and tried to hide from Him. Only praise and sincere worship reopen our relationship with God—through the power of the Holy Spirit and the blood and redemption of the cross.

Lord, I praise You and thank You for anything that today brings. I desire to enter into Your presence.

When you are in God's presence, He knows your faith. Are you prepared to face God with the faith you have? Do you desire to have more faith? Ask our Lord for his help!

Psalm 94:18-19 "When I say, 'My foot is slipping,'/ your love, LORD, holds me up;/ When cares increase within me,/ your comfort gives me joy."

Have you ever walked on a tight rope? If you have, then you may have experienced physical fear. Fear really takes over if your foot slips. At this point, something else takes over that sustains you. You reach deep within yourself to achieve peace and keep your balance.

With the Lord, you never need to worry about slipping. When it occurs, and when you trust in Jesus, He takes over your walk. Yes, then the peace of the Lord takes over.

Lord, thank You for always being there when I slip by taking my eyes off you. Thank you for giving me the grace of having faith in You.

When do you find your faith wavering the most? Is it a constant battle for you to stay faithful and trust in Him?

1 John 5: 14 "[W]e have this confidence in him, that if we ask anything according to his will, he hears us. And if we know that he hears us in regard to whatever we ask, we know that what we have asked him for is ours."

There are times when we don't understand why our prayers are not answered. One reason is sin in our life. If we rebel against God, then we are not in His presence. Another factor is that we pray outside of God's will. Our prayer request might be something that God knows will harm us spiritually, and He loves us too much for that to happen.

When we pray in the will of the Lord, we know that our prayer is placed before throne of the Father. Indeed, Jesus is our intercessor! Since the Father and Jesus are one, we have the promise that our prayers will be answered.

Lord, I praise and thank You for teaching me to rely on You for all my needs, met in accordance to Your perfect will.

God's perfect will is not always what you are hoping for. Do you find it difficult to face this challenge? Do you open your heart to His will? Feel great joy when you accept His Perfect will. Ask Him for guidance.

Acts 8:17 "Then they laid hands on them and they received the Holy Spirit."

At times, I think we fail to realize how significant we are to the spiritual growth of our friends, family and those whom we meet. I know God wants us to pray for them on an ongoing basis. Jesus allows us to be a source of encouragement, inspiration and fellowship. At the same time, we need to correct them in love—when the Lord convicts us to do so.

Jesus will also use us to impart His spiritual gifts to His people. It may be the grace for healing, prophecy, wisdom or any other blessing God wants to give His people. We need only to be obedient in our response.

Lord, I thank and praise You for using me to build up Your people and kingdom!

How does praising God, brings great joy to you? Tell the Lord what a positive impact He has been in helping you evangelize His children.

July 26

Galatians 5:16 "I say, then: live by the Spirit and you will certainly not gratify the desire of the flesh."

It doesn't take too long on this planet earth to know a battle is going on. The battle is our spirit—the Holy Spirit when we become Christians—versus the flesh. The flesh wants to focus on pride, being a victim and instant gratification. The spirit is the opposite. It tells us to love unconditionally, pray for others and self-sacrifice.

This battle will rage until death, when the final enemy is defeated. It increases and decreases based upon our willingness to surrender our will to Jesus.

The key to success is recognizing the impossibility of winning without Christ. We can't win on our own because we only try through the flesh. The good news is that Jesus wins for us when we ask Him to take over the battle.

Bless us in time of battle, Lord. Help us to surrender our will to you so that the victory is yours! I praise You for being the God of victory.

Our Father is waiting for you to surrender your will to Him. Are you ready?

John 21:25 "There are also many other things that Jesus did, but if these were to be described individually, I do not think the whole world would contain the books that would be written."

God cannot be put in box, even if we so desperately want to. One area important to me is to never take too seriously those who seem to have all the answers about God. They will tell you the reason why every Scripture was written and what is coming in mankind's future.

A great song we used to sing to our children is called, "God is a Surprise." A verse is, "Surprise, surprise, God is a surprise, it's baffling to the wise." Indeed! Once we don't limit God's miracles, He can do wonders that we never could imagine.

Open my eyes Lord, to see You as a mystery that I can never truly understand, but still praise and worship You in awe and reverence.

Do you believe your Almighty Father has the power to perform the impossible? What is your struggle in this? Is your faith at the level to believe in His miracles? Without your faith, God won't act. You must believe!

Isaiah 9:5 "They name him Wonder-Counselor, God-Hero,/ Father-Forever, Prince of Peace."

The names of God are an extremely important element of praise. When we acknowledge who He is, we then have fear, which is the beginning of all wisdom. We enter into His presence by praising Him according to His attributes.

This is a reason why, in the Old Testament, there was so much concern about naming God. This was to better understand how to worship Him. I believe that God gives us greater insight into His love for us as we praise the many wondrous things He is for us.

God, you are my everything, my Savior, Redeemer, Prince of Peace, Counselor. I praise You for all things!

In recognizing these attributes, praise God for His many divine manifestations in life. Do you praise God for who He is?

Judges 6:14 "'Go with the strength you have and save Israel from the power of Midian. It is I who send you.'"

God's miracles are ready to work in your life. Are you a Gideon? Gideon was the smallest and least significant member of his family. He also was not trusting of God, because he focused on what he knew versus what God knew as reality. Yet, it was Gideon's faith that ultimately determined the salvation of Israel against superior force.

When God sends us, we need not fear anything. He goes before us to prepare the way to victory. He strengthens us and gives us the tools to defeat the enemy. Even though there may be fantastic odds against us, God will prevail in our lives!

I praise You Lord, for sending me into battle as Your servant.

Do you believe God is there protecting you? Ask Him to send a legion of angels to protect you in your time of need. Recognize God's power and His ongoing protection. Praise Him!

Psalm 29:11 "May the LORD give strength to his people;/ may the LORD bless his people with peace!"

One of the most important aspects of the Christian walk is to realize God's grace is necessary to do anything productive. It is this grace that gives us the strength to do God's will. It also provides us with the peace that only God can bring. When God blesses His people, He provides supernatural intervention in their lives. Miracles begin to occur with both big and small events. Our faith becomes the catalyst for these miracles. As we continue to trust in Him, our strength grows and the peace that passes all understanding takes over.

Lord, I praise You for Your strength and the peace that it provides.

When you let God take over your life, He grants many blessings and miracles. How does your faith build up your relationship with Him? Reflect on how this gives you strength and peace in your faith-filled life.

July 31

Matthew 16:1 "The Pharisees and Sadducees came and, to test him, asked him to show them a sign from heaven."

Where is your faith today? Do you need God to prove Himself to you? Do you need Him to show you a sign of His love? It is interesting that Jesus said that an "evil and unfaithful generation seeks a sign." The lack of faith goes against the will of the Father. Indeed, we know that without faith, it is impossible to please God. With faith, God takes over and blesses our lives.

Teach me, Lord, to rely on You for all things, without needing a sign. I praise You for the gift of wisdom.

True faith doesn't require God to show us signs of wonder. How do you see God acting in your life on a daily basis? While recognizing God greatness, let's take a moment to reflect on the grace of faith that God has given you.

August 1

Luke 1:30 "Then the angel said to her, 'Do not be afraid, Mary, for you have found favor with God.'"

In my experience, you don't usually have to guess where you are with the Lord. He wants you to know without any doubt or uncertainty.

Jesus knows human nature since He was a man for a period of time. He is very much aware that our first emotion is often fear because we can't control the future. However, He very much wants comfort for us and wants to assure us that we are in His favor. When we truly believe, our faith takes over and God begins to work the miracles in our lives that He so richly desires for us.

I praise and thank You, Lord, for blessing us with Your favor.

When you praise and thank God you are deepening your relationship with Him. He sees your heart transform into a heart like His. How does this change you?

Proverbs 12:25 "Anxiety in a man's heart depresses it,/ but a kindly word makes it glad."

I once had a boss who told me there are two kinds of people in the world—those that give anxiety and those that receive it. Which one are you likely to be today? Obviously, we would prefer not to give anxiety or do anything to stress others. Our choices include not receiving anything negative into our spirit. If we are attacked, we can rebuke it and pray extra hard to be in God's presence. The key can be found in our praise and worship. By seeking Him, we block the enemy's darts.

In addition, we can decrease the anxiety we may impart to others by giving them kind words. It is important not to do anything that engenders scandal through conversation or gossip. Our mission is the buildup of the body of Christ by thought, word and deed.

Lord, use me today to build up Your body. May my words be sweet incense unto You. I praise You for giving me the gift of encouragement.

Have you ever had an experience in which you were able to love someone to the point they felt comforted and less anxious? Do you recognize this act as helping build the Body of Christ?

Jonah 2:3 "Out of my distress I called to the LORD,/ and he answered me;/ From the midst of the nether world I cried for help,/ and you heard my voice."

There are times in life when we feel like giving up. Perhaps you are feeling down about how your life is working out.

Expectations are not being met. Don't give up!

The secret is calling out to God from the bottom of your heart. Ask Him to take over your life or a specific situation. Tell Him that without Him, you can do nothing. Then wait and watch for the miracles. Believe in One who created you— and believe in yourself!

I praise and thank You Lord for hearing my voice and answering my needs, according to your perfect will.

Do you rely on the Lord's ability to provide miracles in your life? Do you expect them as you rely on His perfect will? You need to expect and believe in God's power to allow miracles to happen in your life.

Isaiah 45:1 "Thus says the LORD to his anointed, Cyrus,/ whose right hand I grasp...."

I love this story. In a million years, I doubt the Jews would have picked Cyrus as their redeemer, God's instrument who would bring them back from Babylon to Israel. Yet that is just what happened. Cyrus, the king of Persia, the nonbeliever, was picked to be their champion.

So many times in our lives the unexpected happens. We think God has forgotten us or has a certain plan for us. Often, that is just the opposite of what He is thinking and wanting to do. I believe that is why Jesus told us not to worry about tomorrow. Why speculate on something that is unpredictable?

Praise Him for today and hope for tomorrow.

Thank You for bringing people into my life that I don't expect. I praise You for putting them in my life for my blessing.

Do you find that when you are expecting God to act in one way, He performs even greater events in your life? Do you find He places the "right" people in your life at the most crucial and decisive moments?

1 Corinthians 13:7 "It bears all things, believes all things, hopes all things, endures all things."

Love is the greatest of the spiritual gifts. It is eternal and everlasting. Since God is love, when we love others, we bring more of God into our lives.

Love is, indeed, patient and understanding. It is the fruit of the Holy Spirit. Love endures pain and hardship. It believes all things will work out according to the will of the Father. Love is the foundation of hope. As we go forward today and every day, ask the Lord how you can increase the love of God, others and yourself.

Lord, I praise You for teaching me to love Your people as You love me.

Loving God's people with His love is the greatest thing you can do to show God you love Him. It is the true meaning of your life. Reflect: How do you love God's people on a daily basis?

Matthew 5:3 "Blessed are the poor in spirit,/ for theirs is the kingdom of heaven."

Traditionally, the "poor in spirit" are those without material possessions and whose confidence is totally in God. At times our focus may only be on the idea of material possessions rather than on the "
dependence of God.

A number of years ago, I visited a shrine in Paris where I had a very spiritual experience. As I was praying, I "heard" God say to me, "I will give you the gift of poverty." Immediately, my flesh took over. I felt like asking for clarification. Perhaps I had misunderstood. I didn't want to be like the rich man who was afraid to give up his material possessions and follow Jesus.

I made a commitment to give up anything that gets in the way of Jesus. This verse has tremendous power. Indeed, the first step toward entering the kingdom is to be poor in spirit. To be with God, we need total dependence on Him in all things, not only monetary.

I praise You for teaching me to become poor in spirit so that I can receive Your blessings.

Ask the Lord to help you live in His Spirit. Trust Him.

1 Samuel 10:6 "The spirit of the Lord will rush upon you, and you will join them in their prophetic state and you will be changed into another man."

When we accept Christ in our lives, we become a new creation in Him. We literally become a different person. We take on a new identity as sons and daughters of the King. We then have the ability to seek His face and abide in His blessed presence; we receive the favor and grace of the Lord.

Most of us put God in a box. We limit His miracles based upon our limited thinking. When Samuel poured oil on the head of Saul, the anointing of the Lord took over; it was only the sin in Saul's life that brought him pain and suffering.

Blessed be our Lord and Savior, who has redeemed and anointed me with the oil of salvation. I praise You for blessing me.

In your daily living, in what category do you put God? Is He your last-ditch effort in problem solving? Do you keep Him in your pocket hidden and bring Him out only in times of petition? Is this what God' wants?

2 Timothy 2:16 "Avoid profane, idle talk, for such people will become more and more godless."

An occasional profane word! Gossip! Crude humor! No harm, right? Unfortunately, that is exactly what Satan wants you to think—"everybody does it."

God's ways are very specific. We are to use our words for praise and worship and for building up His people. As we strive for holiness, we must realize the "little things" make a big difference. If we fail in our speech, we let the enemy into our lives. Let's reflect back a few weeks or months and see how many times we've fallen.

Lord, may I take seriously every word out of my mouth. May they be as sweet incense unto You. I praise You for taking over my speech and my life.

Do you take the Lord's commandments lightly? Do you stand firm in your faith and honor the Lord with only words that build up His body of Christ?

Psalm 42:3 "Athirst is my soul for God, the living God./ When shall I go and behold the face of God?"

The very essence of our being wants to please God. Our desire is to be reunited with Him; it is the only truly important thing in our lives. As in an arid desert, we seek and thirst for God. To behold the face of God, in the Hebrew sense, is to be in the temple with Him, to experience His presence in the "Holiest of Holies." It is to be reconnected with Him in our spirit. The way to do this is through praise and worship. Praise opens the door for His purifying grace to cleanse us from our sins. As we worship Him, the peace and joy of the Lord fills us.

Lord, I thirst for Your presence in my life. I love You. I praise You for satisfying my thirst.

Do you want to feel His joy and peace in your heart? What must you do? You must praise Him, empty yourself and let Him fill you up with His love. This in turn brings you joy and peace in your heart. Are you ready to do this?

Hebrews 2:18 "Because he himself was tested through what he suffered, he is able to help those who are being tested."

We tend to believe that we're the only ones going through problems and challenges. No one else has had job, marriage, teenager or health problems like ours.

While Jesus did not experience our specific problems, He also was tempted, driven into the desert, abandoned and unappreciated. How did He respond? Jesus loved with all His heart, soul, mind and strength. He forgave His tormentors and enemies.

Jesus, help me to respond to life's challenges as You did. I praise You for giving me Your strength.

Reflect on Jesus' suffering and how He, through the greatest suffering allowed for Him, can aid you and save you in your suffering. Does this give you strength to never give up? Do you understand why you must praise Him? He is always there in your suffering.

Psalm 51:6 "'Against you only I sinned,/ and done what is evil in your sight'..."

David's famous psalm was written after God sent Nathan, the prophet, to confront David about his sin with Bathsheba. David realized his sin was not as much against his fellow man, but was a rebellion against God.

When I sin, I often apologize to whomever I hurt. However, I usually forget the true depth of my rebellion. In full view of my Savior, my Redeemer, I rebelled with selfishness and, therefore, deserve retribution. However, God is merciful and kind. He will forgive me when I come to Him in repentance.

When we rebel against God, we put ourselves outside His grace. When we rebel, we damage our relationship with God. The good news is that we can ask Him for forgiveness. If we come to Him, He will forgive and purify our hearts.

Lord, forgive my rebellion and wash me whiter than snow. I praise You for Your mercy.

We are so fortunate to have the Sacrament of Reconciliation. It is truly a gift. How often do you receive the Sacrament of Reconciliation?

Romans 2:1 "For by the standard by which you judge another you condemn yourself, since you, the judge, do the very same things."

Have you ever known someone who just seems to rub you the wrong way?

With this conflict, everything you do or they do feels wrong. It is usually because there are traits in them that you don't like about yourself. Therefore, when you judge them, you are really "casting sentence" on yourself. Repent and forgive and you will be forgiven!

When you forgive those who trespass against you, you are being Christ-like. If you want to be forgiven, you must forgive. If you seek what is good in people and focus on their goodness, you will find peace and forgiveness—and your spirit will be transformed!

Lord, teach me to have a forgiving spirit in the same way that You have forgiven me. I praise You for giving me a forgiving spirit.

Who is God asking you to forgive? Don't delay! Today is the day of forgiveness!

Psalm 112:1 "Happy the man who fears the LORD,/ who greatly delights in his commands."

Fearing the Lord is the realization of who God is and who we are in comparison. We begin to understand more fully the concept of "fearing" God. Moreover, we finally grasp the fact that without God we can do nothing. Outside of God's grace, our works are but filthy rags.

The laws of the Lord and the Ten Commandments were not written to be burdensome or to prevent our happiness. They were written to protect us from our own sinful nature and ourselves. When we delight in the Lord, He delights in us and provides His blessings. Know that when you come to the Lord, He will bless you for all eternity!

Lord, I praise Your name for loving me so much and for providing Your law for my protection.

Have you ever thought of God's law as a blessing? It is one way He helps bring us to His kingdom. Where have you experienced the blessings of His commandments in your life?

Jeremiah 30:17 "For I will restore you to health;/ of your wounds, I will heal you, says the LORD...."

Jesus is our healer and our only healer. Only through His grace can healing occur. The devil counterfeits healing, but it never lasts. Through the strife and suffering of Jesus, and through His redemption, we can claim His healing promises and Scriptures.

We need not despair when physical illness, depression or any other malady strikes us. It is critical to "stand" on God's Word and claim his promises. He will restore our health and bind our wounds.

Through God the Father, Jesus and the power of the Holy Spirit, you can take authority over sickness in Jesus' name. Jesus will decide how we are to be healed. You must believe in Him and give praise, knowing that you will be healed according to His perfect will.

Lord, thank You for healing me of my thoughts, words, deeds, physical and emotional problems, or anything else that needs grace. I love You and praise Your Holy name!

What are your thoughts on taking that kind of action in your own life?

Psalm 68:12 "The Lord gives the word;/ women bear the glad tidings, a vast army."

I appreciate women for how the Lord uses them. They are often the individuals who lead men into salvation and the heavenly kingdom. Women are compassionate, gentle and loving. They bring life into the world. Indeed, they are the center of life and usually of families.

However, the most important role of women is to announce, "Glad Tidings." In the Old Testament, the Israelite women took an active part in celebrating victories. Today, Christian women play a critical role in celebrating the victory of Christ over sin and death. They bring the "Good News" to their family, friends and those with whom they associate during their activities.

Lord, please bless all women, especially those closest to me. I praise You for my wife, daughter and other women you have put in my life.

What women in your life bring glad tidings, the Good News? Do you praise God for them?

Matthew 24:35 "Heaven and earth will pass away, but my words will not pass away."

Praise the Lord for all things, especially His Word! I believe that if we knew the importance of Scripture, we would read it daily and memorize His promises.

His Word is eternal. It is interesting to note that even heaven and earth will pass away, but the Word will never cease. God will never retract His Word, and it never returns void.

Jesus is incapable of changing His promises. Claim them today!

Lord, thank You for blessing me with Your eternal Word and all the promises contained in it. I praise You for Your Word.

How important is His Word in your life? How often do you read Scripture?

Nahum 1:9 "The enemy shall not rise a second time."

There are seasons for everything. I believe, at times, God may take His hand off us and allow the enemy to win some battles. Why? Doesn't He always love us?

It is important to remember, like any good father, Jesus wants to shape and mold us. He wants to cleanse us of our rebellion. While God is merciful, He is also just. He will heal our wounds and straighten our paths when we repent and turn to Him to take over our lives.

The enemy will try to convince you that God has abandoned you. Don't believe it! God will never abandon you. By His blood, you are saved and your bondage has been broken for all eternity. Indeed, the enemy will not win or rise again in your life when you trust Jesus!

Lord, I praise and thank You for Your blessings and grace against all evil.

Do you ever fall into darkness and think God isn't there? Erase those thoughts from your mind. God the Father is greater than your thinking or feelings—and far greater than the evil one. Do you put your faith in Him and praise Him for His blessings and grace against evil?

Revelation 22:20 "...'Yes, I am coming soon.' Amen! Come, Lord Jesus!"

Our return to the Lord Jesus Christ is right around the corner. We need not be afraid or fear! Jesus has broken the chains of death and sin—and has redeemed us. Rejoice!

Today, many people focus on "end times." They believe in the rapture of the church and feel it is coming soon. While there are many opinions on the end times, there is one thing I know. Our life is but a vapor that appears briefly and disappears. Furthermore, Jesus is coming soon for us, whether or not we want to think about it.

Lord, come quickly to us, as we desire to be with you for all of eternity, always praising Your holy name! I praise You for breaking my bondage.

Can you imagine living eternally with our Lord? Do you live in fear for the end of times or are you preparing for His return? Do not fear, for God has the perfect plan!

Luke 14:11 "For everyone who exalts himself will be humbled, but the one who humbles himself will be exalted."

If you reflect on how the world conditions our behavior, it is obvious this verse is the exact opposite of what is usually desired. Most of the time, getting positions of authority, being in power, wanting to be seen as the expert or the best is the usual course of action. We look at athletes, such as Muhammad Ali, who said, "I am the greatest!" Then, we do similar things by "trash talking our way through life."

Jesus is the role model of humility. Despite being God, He humbled Himself and became human so that we could be saved. He asks us not to be proud in this world, but to give the glory to God.

Lord Jesus, I praise You for teaching me to be humble in all ways—in the same way You were humble.

Do you catch yourself being prideful and becoming, in effect, your own god? Can you think of ways in which you can be humbler before the Lord and serve only Him?

Acts 2:46 "Every day they devoted themselves to meeting together in the temple area and to breaking bread in their homes. They ate their meals with exaltation and sincerity of heart."

We were not created to be alone. We were created to be in community. We were connected to God even before we were born. As Christians, we are part of the "body of Christ," which is a community of believers.

"How do you spend your time?" Do you associate with a community of believers who love the Lord? Are they like a family for you? Do you spend quality time with them, including sharing meals?

Two key words in today's verse are "every day." This is not getting together once in a while, but making it a priority. Allowing believers into our lives holds us accountable for our spiritual growth. In also being vulnerable to each other, we can confidently share and acknowledge our struggles and shortfalls.

Lord, send to me a community of believers so that I can share my life with them. I praise You for my parish and prayer community.

How can you better serve God by serving His people?

Genesis 1:31 "God looked at everything he had made, and he found it very good."

Praise the Lord! God looked at all He had made and found it good. Did He make you? Are you His creation? I hope you don't think a few arbitrary atoms got together to form you. Indeed, God created you for His purpose— to praise Him for all eternity. By praising Him, you enter into His presence and receive our Lord's blessings. You cannot be in God's presence unless you are holy.

For most of us, I believe the biggest area for inner healing can be found in our poor self-esteem. We simply don't think we are worthy of anything good. In a sense, that is true; we are sinners. But, Jesus rectified that with the cross. We are good and are created to do good works. Don't let the devil fool you into thinking you are junk. As they say in Marriage Encounter, "God doesn't make junk!"

I praise You for making me good, Lord Jesus, due to Your death on the cross.

Reflect on the fact that you are part of His perfect will. God is going to use you to bring His glory to earth. In turn, you will receive everlasting life.

John 13:8 "...'Unless I wash you, you will have no inheritance with me.'"

This verse occurs in Scripture when Jesus asks to wash the feet of Peter. Peter, of course, as only he can, doesn't understand and thinks he is doing the noble thing by refusing Jesus. However, Jesus tells Peter he will have no future with Him if he doesn't allow Jesus to wash his feet.

What does that mean? It means something at many levels. Most importantly, it is a lesson in humility. We can't save ourselves. Only Jesus, by washing us clean of our sins, can save us.

We must become child-like to accept that truth.

Come, Lord Jesus, and accept all of me to be washed by You. I praise You for being the God of humility.

Jesus shows us His humility. Do you follow His example? You must allow Jesus to cleanse your spirit with His love and forgiveness. Do you allow Him to cleanse you? The sacrament of Reconciliation is there!

Psalm 71:1 "In you, O LORD, I take refuge;/ let me never be put to shame."

At what time or circumstance should we take refuge in the Lord? When we feel like it? When we are down and out or in our old age?

The Psalmist in this verse focuses on his advancing age and his relationship with God. He realizes he must trust totally in God's hands. Without Him, he can do nothing.

So many things in our lives can move us away from doing God's will, if we let them. These events or activities can keep us off focus. God clearly is telling us to trust Him, to take refuge in His promises and His Word, and to know that we will never be confused or be put to shame

I praise and thank You Lord for being my refuge and keeping me from shame.

Do you feel God's love and healing power in your life?

Psalm 100:1-2 "Sing joyfully to the LORD, all you lands;/ serve the LORD with gladness;/ come before him with joyful song."

Do you sing joyfully before the Lord? Do you serve Him with gladness? I know I don't, at least to the extent that I would like to. Singing joyfully with all our heart is one of the best ways of praising God. As St. Augustine once said, "When you sing before the Lord, you are praying twice."

God is love and the fruits of that love are joy, peace and hope. Joy occurs as we enter the presence of God. This presence is achieved through sincere worship, often through singing. It is not a coincidence that most church services include music as a major part of worship. Unfortunately, all too many times, the music ministry becomes more like entertainment than the catalyst for individual praise and worship through song. God wants us to individually praise Him with all our heart, mind and strength. Often this is best expressed through singing.

Thank you, Lord, for giving us the gift of music. May we always praise You through joyful song, which arises from our hearts and rejoices on our lips.

Do you sing to the Lord with all your heart and soul?

August 25

James 1:27 "Religion that is pure and undefiled before God and the Father is this: to care for orphans and widows in their affliction and to keep oneself unstained by the world."

You have to love St. James and his writing. James always said exactly what he was thinking, never mincing his words. If you didn't do what he thought should happen, he made sure his writings reflected his" opinion.

In this Scripture passage, James is saying that we can't call ourselves pure without taking care of those around us in need. In the Old Testament, orphans and widows were usual examples of the defenseless or oppressed. Today, it is still our duty to watch over the lonely, the oppressed and those without hope, to offer aid either financially or with our time and talent.

Lord, make me an example of Your peace, while I actively assist Your people in need. I praise You for using me to build up Your kingdom.

Do you see all people as the children of God? Do you treat them with His love or your love of the flesh? In what ways do you love with His love? In what ways do you ignore Him and His children?

2 Peter 1:20-21 "Know this first of all, that there is no prophecy of scripture that is a matter of personal interpretation, for no prophecy ever came through human will; but rather human beings moved by the holy Spirit spoke under the influence of God."

I have often said the Bible is God's instruction manual for living. For you football fans, it is God's play-by-play book. I have played many a board game over the years. I wouldn't think of playing a new game without reading the rules.

Why do we think we can go through life without knowing God's rule book? We would think it is silly to play a game by our own rules and then think that we could win. Yet, we do exactly that when we ignore God's laws. It is like pretending the law of gravity doesn't exist.

God inspired and created Scripture through man so that we could learn how to lead our lives. The commandments are not punishment, but daily provisions for our own protection.

I praise Your name for giving me the life-giving Bible.

Do you rejoice in the Good News of the Bible?

Acts 13:52 "The disciples were filled with joy and the holy Spirit."

Do you have joy in your life? Perhaps you're familiar with the song, "The Joy of the Lord is My Strength!" The song's lyrics pronounce that, as a Christian, you need to sing, jump and shout for it. In that way, joy becomes a verb; you actively seek God's presence through your praise and thanksgiving, which often overflows into song.

When you have the joy of the Lord, there is no doubt. The disciples felt it every day. And, through the indwelling of the Holy Spirit, they faithfully followed God's will. As long as they trusted God, joy was present.

Lord, may I seek Your face and receive Your joy each and every day. I praise You for the gift of joy.

Do you belong to a prayer group that sings and praises God? This is an important part of loving God. Go forth and find what you need to praise Him.

Acts 14:3 "So they stayed for a considerable period, speaking out boldly for the Lord, who confirmed the word about his grace by granting signs and wonders to occur through their hands."

The disciples were active in their ministry; likewise, we are to be active in our ministry of building God's Kingdom. Can you imagine where we all would be today if the disciples wanted to keep their faith private? Did they say it was between "them and God?" Of course not! Our faith is one of community, reaching out to one another.

When we are in touch with God's will, signs and wonders occur in a big way. Today, many of God's signs and wonders are happening in South America, Africa and Asia.

Lord Jesus, open my eyes to see Your truth, so that Your miracles can flow through me. I praise Your holy name.

Do you fear sharing your faith in an outward way? Do not be afraid; God is there before you and will bless your efforts when you speak of His truth. Does knowing this give you courage to act? Be courageous for the Lord?

Psalm 41:4 "The LORD will help him on his sickbed,/ he will take away all his ailments when he is ill."

Do we believe God heals? Do we believe God heals us when we ask Him? Scripture proclaims that "all things will work for our good, if we are called according to His holy will."

We also know that if we ask anything of the Father in the name of Jesus, it will be granted to us—if we are in His will.

It seems impossible to accurately ask "in the name of Jesus" without being holy and connected to Him. If we are not, our prayers are not answered. Why? Because we are not in the divine presence of God or in tune with His will. If we were, we would jump up from our sick bed and rejoice in all His blessings.

Lord, I thank You for healing my sickness by Your dying on the cross for my sins and diseases. I praise You for the gift of healing.

Do you believe God can perform miracles through you? Reflect on your openness regarding the healing of people in your life. Would God want you to be the catalyst that heals people with God's love?

Mark 6:12-13 "So they went off and preached repentance. They drove out many demons, and they anointed with oil many who were sick and cured them."

This passage is from the great commission Jesus gave to His disciples. They went out into the country, spreading the Word of Jesus. That message is the same message we need to receive today: repentance. For us to want a Savior, we must believe that we need to be saved.

What do we need to be saved of? Our sins! That message is a difficult one for most people in this age of relativity. Perhaps you may have heard a talk entitled, "What ever happened to sin?" Today, as in the time of Jesus, we rationalize away our sins; moreover, we don't think we need to repent or put Jesus at the center of our life.

I find it interesting that the healing of people only occurs after the repentance! It tells me that without repentance, we cannot be in the presence of God; therefore, His healing power is not manifested.

Lord, I repent of my sins. I need You both as my Savior and the center of my life.

Are you humble and do you lift your sins up to the Lord? Be humble and repent. Let Jesus heal you of your sins.

1 Thessalonians 5: 14 "We urge you, brothers, admonish the idle, cheer the fainthearted, support the weak, be patient with all."

One of the best aspects of Scripture is its practicality. When you think that these passages were written almost 2,000 years ago, it is pretty amazing.

Paul is telling us today, as he told the Thessalonians, to let the "freeloaders" know that they need to get motivated and get to work. Sloth is a serious sin that must be brought to the light! Also, those who need encouragement because they are fearful need our support. Also, people who are without means or incapable of independence, need our assistance. Finally, patience with each other is always critical for the Christian walk.

Thank you, Lord, for teaching me how to live in this world according to your precepts. I praise You for Your grace.

Do you prioritize God above all things? Ask the Lord to give you the grace to offer Him your whole heart, mind, body and soul for His glory.

1 Thessalonians 5:16-18 "Rejoice always. Pray without ceasing. In all circumstances give thanks, for this is the will of God for you in Christ Jesus."

You have to love St Paul. He cuts to the core when instructing Christians how to live out their lives. "Rejoice always." Always? You've got to be kidding? Rejoice when I'm sick or depressed or lost my job? Rejoice when my kids or spouse is yelling at me? Absolutely! Rejoicing shows our trust in God and our belief that all things will work for good; we love Him and desire to live according to His will. Thus, we give thanks in "all things."

Praying without ceasing seems an impossible task. Indeed, in the flesh it is, but with God everything is possible. Why? Because when we do His will, we are living a life of prayer. We are in harmony with the Lord; and we are praising Him in everything we do and say— our thoughts, words and actions. Thus, we live a life of prayer.

I praise You Jesus for all things in my life, and I rejoice in my salvation.

Do you praise God for who He is? It is high form of prayer.

Proverbs 1:7 "The fear of the LORD is the beginning of knowledge;/ wisdom and instruction fools despise."

What does it mean to fear the Lord? Indeed, some theologians feel the foundation of all Christianity is the fear of the Lord. When we think of fear, it usually is a negative emotion. However, reverential fear is respecting God for His sovereignty, mercy and justice with us. It is the acknowledgement of who God is and who we are in respect to Him.

When we fear God, we grow in wisdom. Without this fear, we often respond in foolish ways and faulty thinking. Thus, we make poor decisions and often think we are like gods in all that we accomplish. It is then that our pride takes us down, and we fall from grace.

Lord, I pray that I continually fear and love You according to Your will and plan for my life. I praise You for the gift of wisdom.

Do you put the Lord first in your heart? If you don't, yet long for it, you must first empty yourself of your want. Then, fill yourself with His love and acceptance. Do you believe you will feel the joy in "doing His perfect will?

Leviticus 19: 8 "You shall love your neighbor as yourself."

Most of us don't realize that this saying occurs not only in the New Testament, but in the Old Testament as well. What does it mean for us today? At the time it was written, the emphasis was on the "children" of Israel, the Israelites. However, Jesus later expanded the verse to include everyone.

There have been times in my life when I struggled with this saying. It was not because I didn't want to love others, but the reality was I didn't love myself as much as I desired. It is important to reflect on the fact that God's divine life is instilled in each of us when we are baptized. We start a new sacramental commitment and relationship with Jesus. God is within us. And, because we are imbued with this grace, we are to love our neighbor as God loves us.

Thank you, Lord, for giving me the grace to love others as You love us. I praise You for being the God of love.

Have you heard throughout your life about "loving thy neighbor?" Do you ever try looking into the heart of the individual? They may be suffering, and when you love them with the Father's love, God can heal them!

Deuteronomy 6:5 "Therefore, you shall love the LORD, your God, with all your heart, and with all your soul, and with all your strength."

This is the "great commandment." God doesn't want a little of us. He doesn't want the crumbs or leftovers. God wants the entire seven-course meal. He wants all of us, including our hopes, dreams, fears, anxieties and anything else we have to offer. I believe that is how we can love God with all of our heart and soul.

This offering, this living, loving sacrifice of ourselves is what we give with all of our strength. It is the hope for the future. It is the belief that God loves us so much that our future is a guaranteed blessing.

Lord, teach me how to love You with all my heart, soul and strength. I praise You for giving me Your strength, Your Holy Spirit.

Do you find God as you pray? Do you practice deep, contemplative prayer? He teaches you how to love Him with your whole heart. Did you know prayer is the tool to loving God with your whole heart, soul and strength?

John 3:16 "For God so loved the world that he gave his only Son, so that everyone who believes in him might not perish but might have eternal life."

This widely known verse in John is the embodiment of Christianity. God *is* love. The Father, Jesus and the Holy Spirit *are* love. The eternal Word becoming flesh and dying for our sins manifested that love.

If you were God, would you give up heaven and come to earth to die on a cross? And, would you want to suffer a painful, horrific death? Most of us wouldn't do anything even remotely close to that for those we love the most, let alone for complete strangers. However, God gave us a perfect model, Jesus, who testified to the depth of His Father's love for all of us. He will do anything for us, if we just say "Yes" to His love.

Lord, Jesus, I say yes to Your love! I thank You and praise You for dying for me and redeeming me.

How do you say yes to God's love and mean it? Do you value the sacrifice of His son, Jesus, because of His love for you?

John 13:34 "'I give you a new commandment: love one another. As I have loved you, so you also should love one another.'"

To love as Jesus loves is very difficult. Is it impossible No! However, we would be incapable of that kind of love without the grace of Jesus.

I believe that is why Jesus said it is impossible to do anything without Him. Therefore, we must ask that Jesus' love enter our hearts, and His love to flow into our empty vessel. Then, upon receiving God's living and eternal waters of love, God's overflowing love will spill over to others we encounter.

Many people complain they are incapable of loving themselves, their spouse or families in the way they want. What they don't understand is love is a gift, in the same way faith is a gift. To receive this gift, we must ask for it and expect that we will receive it, because it is guaranteed!

Thank you, Jesus, for the gift of love! I praise You for loving me unconditionally.

Is it hard to accept how weak you are without Jesus' love? Can you try to love as He loves? Draw closer to Him so you can truly experience that love.

John 14: 15 "'If you love me, you will keep my commandments.'"

Loving God and keeping His commandments can be a troubling thought. Who doesn't sin and fall short of the mark? Fortunately, we have a Savior who washes us whiter than snow and forgives our sins.

When you love someone, you want to be with him or her. That, in the purist sense, is what "keeping the commandments" is all about: remaining in the presence of God at all times.

When we are in relationship with Jesus, through the power of the Holy Spirit, we are not breaking His commandments. As we give Him our praise and worship, we realize the commandments are for our benefit. We give thanks to God for them.

Lord Jesus, I love You and desire to always keep Your commandments. I praise You for Your guidance in my life.

Do you seek Jesus's guidance and follow Him in your heart and with your words and actions? Jesus will help you in your journey following your commandments.

John 14 21b: "'[W]hoever loves me will be loved by my Father, and I will love him and reveal myself to him.'"

The only way to the Father is through the Son. Indeed, we "know" the Father when we have a relationship with Jesus. How do we discover the joy of being one with Jesus? When we ask Him into our heart in a loving way. Since Jesus is love, when we love Him, we become connected to His being and presence through the power of the Holy Spirit. We want more of Him, in the same way that we want more of anyone we love.

That is the same with Jesus. Realizing that He has always loved us, our eyes are opened. We feel His presence throughout our life and hear His loving voice.

Thank You Lord, for loving me and bringing me to the Father. I praise You for all things.

Do you let Jesus guide you to the Father so that you may enter the kingdom of heaven? If we follow Jesus, we will receive the greatest reward—everlasting life. Do you listen to the Holy Spirit, follow the ways of Jesus and ask our mother, Mary, for her intercession?

September 9

Psalm 9:10 "The LORD is a stronghold for the oppressed,/ a stronghold in times of distress."

Do you feel discouraged today? Usually, it's because our plan is not working out.

We have been promised trials and persecution in this world. However, we've also been promised that we'll never be abandoned. God, indeed, will be our stronghold, if we just let Him! When we trust Him, He is there to give us peace, joy and hope.

I know, for me, when I feel oppressed, it is usually when my expectations of a perfect life are not evident. When I realize that my ways are not God's ways, then I am back on track. As I totally surrender to Jesus, He becomes my stronghold.

Lord, I praise and thank You for being my stronghold in difficult times.

Do you focus on the Lord's love in difficult times? If not, what keeps you from holding onto Him? Lack of faith?

September 10

Judges 18:5-6 "They said to him, 'Consult God that we may know whether the undertaking we are engaged in will succeed.' The priest said to them, 'Go and prosper: the LORD is favorable to the undertaking you are engaged in.'"

In our life, God provides us answers when we ask Him. The answer might be to wait on Him until He is ready to act. I believe the Lord often delays His answers to build up our patience and faith. If He acted too soon, we might not have the opportunity to grow. Therefore, praise God in all things, even patience!

I firmly believe Jesus wants us to prosper. However, our definition of "prosper" may not be the same as God's. For the Lord, to prosper is to grow spiritually. As an afterthought, the Lord might bless us materially, if it fits into our growth. Our material wealth only becomes a priority when it can be used for building up the kingdom.

Lord, I praise Your name for the life battles I am in now. I know I will prosper according to Your perfect will. I praise You for Your strength in me through the power of the Holy Spirit.

Do you find it difficult to praise God during your battles? Praising Him is essential, you will endure with His aid!

September 11

Isaiah 54: 15 "Should there be any attack, it shall not be of my making;/ whoever attacks you shall fall before you."

Today is the anniversary of the horrific attack on our country by terrorists. Many people are still living in fear. They fear flying, the future or, in general, an even worse attack.

I believe God doesn't want a spirit of fear or a country that lives in fear. I know God wants us to trust in Him and have faith that we will be protected. This verse reaffirms that the attack is not of God's making, and whoever attacks us will not be successful.

Our country is stronger than ever, despite the terror. We are more determined to live in God's will. It is critical that we pray for wisdom, grace and protection for our leaders and country.

God Bless America today and always! Amen! I praise You for our country.

How do you find strength to endure such a tragedy?

Ephesians 1:4-5 "[A]s he chose us in him, before the foundation of the world, to be holy and without blemish before him. In love, he destined us for adoption to himself through Jesus Christ, in accord with the favor of his will."

Do you see yourself as holy and without blemish? I'm sure most of us, at some level, are saying, "You have got to be kidding!" Without blemish? That lasted 30 seconds after I was born! However, this is how God sees you. The reason? His death on the cross cleansed us from our sins, so that in the eyes of Jesus you are pure and holy.

Meditate on how much Jesus loves you. You are precious for all of eternity. You have been cleansed by the blood of the lamb! Rejoice and claim your inheritance as adopted children of Jesus!

Did you know God's perfect way is what allows Him to see us only as unblemished? If we saw ourselves as perfect, you wouldn't strive very hard to be like Jesus or to sacrifice as Jesus did for us. Our faults allow us to grow in God's love.

Lord, I praise Your name for creating me in Your image and with Your sacrifice, making me holy.

He has forgiven you? Do you see yourself being holy?

Isaiah 46:11cd "Yes, I have spoken, I will accomplish it;/ I have planned it, and I will do it."

God listens to every prayer. He wants to fill us with His Spirit and gifts. He doesn't want us miserable. Most of all, God wants us to receive the grace and blessings He has in store for us. If we rebel, He is faithful and will take the time needed for us to learn our lesson. Repent of your rebellion and allow the Lord to fulfill His plan for you! God will do it, in His time.

Lord, teach me obedience and patience to wait on Your plan. I praise You for Your correction and love.

His way is not always what you want. Are you sacrificing your own desires to be obedient to the Lord? Are you aware that the "fruit" of patience occurs when you trust and believe in God and His plan and timing for your life?

1 Corinthians 13:13 "So faith, hope, love remain, these three; but the greatest of these is love."

I went to a teaching recently at a conference on the subject of afterlife experiences. After surveying many near-death events, the consistent theme that emerged, according to the speaker, was the reality that the love you have in your heart when you die is the same love you take into the next life.

Why? Because God is love. It stands to reason the only aspect of life that makes sense to continue is the treasure of loving and knowing love, which is Jesus. The love that is in our hearts is the foundation we take into the next world. God will honor that because He is honoring Himself!

Jesus, teach me to love You and Your people in the way You desire. I love You!

Do you read the Bible and focus on the Scriptures that tell you of Jesus' love? Did you know the hope He brought to the sinful, the sick, the lost, the broken and the sorrowful is inspiring and helps you to better understand Jesus?

Matthew 6:20 "But store up treasures in heaven, where neither moth nor decay destroys, nor thieves break in and steal."

How can we store up anything in heaven? I know you can only store something that is in your possession—things you own.

What "possessions" can we take with us into the next eternal life? Which part of us is God in? The answer to both is love!

It is the love we have for God and for others that is carried with us for all eternity as Christians. Love is the treasure that will be built and made to shine like the stars when we are with the Lord in heaven.

Lord, teach me only to seek the treasure that is everlasting—Your love which permeates my soul! I praise You for the gift of love!

Look into all the crevices of your heart, your being. Are you willing to welcome God into every part of your life? The more love you have the more of Him is in you. What joy!

1 John 4:7 "Beloved, let us love one another, because love is of God; everyone who loves is begotten by God and knows God."

As sons and daughters of God, we are heirs to His grace and power. When we ask Jesus into our hearts, it is His love that transforms us into His image. With this transformation, we use the living waters within us to well up with the love of Jesus. This love thus flows out of us to others.

Is it possible to love others without the grace of Jesus? No! It is through His power that we love at all. Through God's grace, we receive His gift of love and better understand His attributes, thereby helping us to be God's ambassador to others. Love becomes the key fruit in our lives because God loved us first and helped us transform that love into action toward our brothers and sisters.

Help me, Lord, to love one another as You love me. I praise You for all things!

Is it difficult to love others as He loves you? Remember His love is in you when you welcome Him in. Share that love!

1 John 4:19 "We love because he first loved us."

Most of us think we are in charge of choosing to love or not to love. However, the truth is that because God loved us first, we are able to receive His love. We then can reflect that love to others.

I strongly suggest meditating on this verse. The spiritual reality is that God loves us unconditionally. This truth will transform our lives if we allow it to. We will receive His grace because God wants to give every gift to His children.

Lord, I praise Your name and thank You for Your unconditional love.

Do you look to the saints, especially Mary our blessed Mother? They show great love. This love was possible because of their trust and faith in the Lord.

1 John 3:17 "If someone who has worldly means sees a brother in need and refuses him compassion, how can the love of God remain in him?"

The social justice Gospel often can trouble us because it makes us feel guilty. We feel like we should do more. John tells us to keep our eyes open for opportunities to help others. If those around us are in need and we close our eyes and heart, it is because we are in love with the world and not Jesus.

I believe God wants us to be compassionate to those that He loves—which is everyone. We cannot refuse to help them because God, in turn, has given us so many great gifts and showered us with His abundant love—in spite of our sinful and unworthy nature. Do not ignore those who have less. We will bring judgment down on ourselves.

Lord, give me a compassionate heart, so that I can serve others. I praise You for the grace to help the poor in spirit and the poor of the world.

Do you struggle with helping the needy? Pray for guidance.

1 John 3:17 "If someone who has worldly means sees a brother in need and refuses him compassion, how can the love of God remain in him?"

I love fruit. I often go to our local farmer's market to purchase fruit grown in local fields—grown longer than what you can buy in the supermarket. This fruit is beautiful and ripe. And, I always know this better fruit by its luscious taste and texture.

In the same way, our fruit is shown by our actions. It is not our words only, but our actions that determine the flavor of our life. It is something pleasing to God? Or is it picked too soon and has no taste? It is up to us. If we allow the Lord to nourish and ripen us through His Word, we will bear the better fruit of the Holy Spirit.

Lord Jesus, ripen us according to Your will, so that we bear fruit that pleases You. I praise You for being the vine in my life.

He nourishes us with His love so that we bear fruit. How do you share the fruit you have been given to build up God's kingdom?

Proverbs 16:9 "In his mind a man plans his course,/ but the LORD directs his steps."

One of my favorite sayings is, "We plan, God laughs." Indeed, most of us have our lives all figured out in our minds. We think we are going to do this and that, and it will all be wonderful!

God knows what path we are on and what path He wants us to be on. He will take care of all our needs. Relax, and enjoy the journey!

Thank You Lord, for directing all my steps. I love you! I praise You now and forever!

Do you recognize that the Holy Spirit is able to guide you in your daily life? Are you thankful to our Lord, for His way will bring you everlasting life in Him?

Proverbs 13:11 "Wealth quickly gotten, dwindles away,/ but amassed little by little, it grows."

In today's society, a get-rich-quick mentality runs rampant. You see it in lottery lines, pyramid schemes, the explosion in gambling across the country and the stock market. How about you? Did you think that success in the stock market or real estate will end your problems?

I believe the desire to get rich or, even worse, to get rich without earning it, is definitely not of the Lord. His desire is for us to grow in holiness, not in our bank account. If we are blessed financially, it is because of a special grace, not because it was our desire.

Lord, may I always focus on building treasure that lasts for all eternity. I praise You for building true treasure in my life.

Whatever your financial circumstances, are you making the choice to be "rich in spirit"? Are you following Him and building an everlasting treasure with the Lord? It's never too late!

Proverbs 16:3 "Entrust your needs to the LORD,/ and your plans will succeed."

Sounds simple, doesn't it? Just trust in God and everything wonderful happens. Since we know life doesn't work like that, what is wrong? The first clue is the word "trust." What does that really mean?

Look at the relationship of Jesus to His Father. Jesus always trusted Him and was obedient to His will. Therefore, whatever work Jesus accomplished was blessed and fulfilled because He was in the will of the Father.

Teach me Lord, to conform to Your will so that my works build Your kingdom. I praise You for choosing me to build Your kingdom!

If you pray for God's help to do His work, do you listen to Him with your heart? Do you realize that you must choose to be obedient to His perfect Will to build His kingdom?

Ephesians 4:26-27 "Be angry but do not sin; do not let the sun set on your anger, and do not leave room for the devil."

I spent much of my life believing that anger was a sin. Even now, I often stuff my feelings because I struggle with "past tapes" that repeat "anger is wrong."

This verse gives freedom to people like me who have struggled with anger. It clearly states that I need to deal with my feelings and "put my anger to bed." Indeed, I need to express my anger openly, but in love, and before I go to sleep. Otherwise, my anger builds and festers in my heart and soul.

Lord, teach me to deal with my anger daily and in love. I praise You for being the God of forgiveness.

Are you following Jesus' way of forgiveness? He expressed His anger and then told the people why He was angry. He would share His love for the Father. Do you?

Psalm 6:10 "The LORD has heard my plea;/ the LORD has accepted my prayer."

God hears every prayer from the faithful and He will act those in His will. He is a loving Father who gently answers us through the whisper of a soft breeze, the vibrant colors of a sunset, or, perhaps, the pounding beauty of the ocean, awash with lively spray and white foam.

How is that an answer? These are some ways through which God expresses "All is well on heaven and earth." Trust in Him and rejoice. We need not be afraid or worry.

Lord, thank You for answering my prayers according to Your perfect will. I praise You for Your love of me and being the God of love.

Do you pray with your "Father's will"? If you pray for His will, you will never be disappointed by His answers.

Luke 12:22 "He said to [his] disciples, 'Therefore I tell you, do not worry about your life and what you will eat, or about your body and what you will wear.'"

Does this sound like us? Do we never worry about anything to do with food or clothing or whether we have the latest designer clothes or, perhaps, what others think about our "look"?

Jesus clearly tells us to focus on the spiritual and not the physical, which will soon pass away. We need to build eternal treasure that won't go "out of fashion." When we do that, the pressures are greatly reduced. It's a poor legacy for our children to be enslaved by fashion or the world.

I praise You, Lord, for Your eternal gifts.

Do you recognize that the gifts of God are the most valuable? Do you struggle with one foot in the world and the other in His Spirit?

1 Samuel 23:4 "Again David consulted the LORD, who answered, "Go down to Keilah, for I will deliver the Philistines into your power."'

Who are the Philistines in your life? As you recall, David was a small, young man going against a mighty army and an unbeaten champion. His first step was to consult with the Lord. Secondly, he listened. And, his final step was action.

The Philistine in my life is fear—fear of not being successful and fear I am inadequate as a husband, father and Deacon. When I confront it, the Lord takes over to give me confidence and peace.

Lord, I praise and thank You for guiding me in defeating the Philistines in my life.

Who are the Philistines in your life? You can use the strength and love of God the Father, to conquer your challenges.

1 Samuel 26:24 "As I valued your life highly today, so may the LORD value my life highly and deliver me from all difficulties."

As we treat and judge people, so does the Lord deal with us. Recently, the Lord put me to the test. A co-worker did something that, by most accounts, was petty and fairly outrageous. I consulted with a friend who suggested that I respond in kind or worse.

However, I felt differently. I felt the Lord wanted me to love this person by showing kindness. I was not being a doormat, but at the same time, I turned the other cheek. The result? The problem was solved in my favor and the relationship healed.

Lord, I praise and thank You for helping me with the challenges in my life.

Do you want to act in His love? You must listen to His loving guidance. Prayer is the answer when you look for His guidance and help in difficult matters.

Psalm 30:13 "**That my soul might sing praise to you without ceasing;/ O LORD, my God, forever will I give you thanks.**"

For what do we give thanks to the Lord? How about everything! Think about being able to get up in morning—alive! How about your health, even if it is not perfect? The many blessings of family and friends, the beauty of God's universe and the grace of giving and receiving love.

God has many blessings for us. That alone is enough to praise Him forever. However, we praise God for who He is and not for what He has done for us. God is love, and we praise Him for being the God of love!

I praise You for being my God, my Healer, my Lord.

God's healing love gives us great reason to praise Him. How have you been healed? Maybe a friend or family member has been healed because of your prayers. Praise Him now and forever!

Psalm 127:1 "Unless the LORD built the house,/ they labor in vain who build it./ Unless the LORD guard the city,/ in vain does the guard keep vigil."

Whatever you are building, unless the Lord builds it, nothing good will come from it. How can we let the Lord build our house? First, we must not make our job, family, ministry or anything else our god. We must not love the success of our ventures more than we love the Lord. Secondly, our love for Jesus must be the foundation of our house, for then, the Holy Spirit builds the framework.

Lord, may You build my life and be my foundation. I praise You for being my house!

What is the foundation of your life made of? Is it God's love? Is it made of things not of God? Your foundation will be on rock and lasting if God is at the core and center of your life!

Proverbs 3:5-6 "Trust in the LORD with all your heart,/ on your intelligence rely not;/ In all your ways be mindful of him,/ and he will make straight your paths."

How many business or motivational books/tapes say, "Don't rely on your intelligence?" Remember, God's ways are not our ways. The path to the Lord is narrow and often difficult to maneuver. We need guidance and help to reach our goal: the Lord. We can't rely on our own power.

When we put our trust in God, the crooked path straightens. And, God then carries us, without our realizing it. So, rejoice and be glad!

Lord, thank You for guiding me into Your kingdom.

In what ways are you following Jesus and working toward His Heavenly Kingdom? Though you may falter at times, keep your heart on Him; He will guide you whenever you veer off His path.

Isaiah 41:13 "For I am the LORD, your God,/ who grasp your right hand;/ It is I who say to you, 'Fear not,/ I will help you.'"

Do you know the words that Jesus spoke the most? "Do not be afraid, fear not!" That is because, for most of us, our lives are full of anxiety and fear. Jesus came to take away that fear. He wants us to live with a sense of peace and joy.

It is important to meditate on this verse. Picture Jesus holding your right hand. He is looking into your face with loving eyes and telling you how much He loves you. Jesus assures us not to be fearful because He is with us for all eternity. Forever, He holds us in the palm of His hand

Lord Jesus, I praise and thank You for grasping my hand and taking away my fear.

How does it feel in your heart that Jesus is always there for you? You just need to ask Him from your heart.

Isaiah 43:19 "See, I am doing something new! / Now it springs forth, do you not perceive it?/ In the desert I make a way,/ in the wasteland, rivers."

The beauty of loving Jesus is seeing each day the new creation in our lives. Look for it! He is doing something new and wonderful every day. Do not grow discouraged. He will give you living waters that will wash away your sinful habits.

Each day is exciting when we look for God's miracles. He is showering us with His grace!

I praise You for being the God of encouragement and strength.

How does our Lord encourage you? Is it through people in your life? Notice how God uses people to encourage and support you.
Praise Him!

Isaiah 48:10 "At the beginning, I foretell the outcome, in advance, things not yet done. I say that my plan shall stand. I accomplish my every purpose."

The will of the Father shall be done without fail! Do not fear or be disheartened if it is not done in your timing. If it were done according to your will, would God be in it?

God has a plan for your life. Do not think twice about it. The real question is, "Do you want His plan or your plan?" What if His plan doesn't fit with your plan? This is the test: "Do you want to build the kingdom, at any cost?" I guarantee you this reality: God's plan will always be the best and give you everlasting peace and joy.

Lord, teach me patience to do Your will and to listen for the plan You have for my life. I praise You for the gift of patience.

Patience will come with the acceptance of His will. Do you trust the Father's judgment regarding what is best for you? If you do, then you can just worry about the present and wait expectantly for His miracles.

Amos 9:15 "I will plant them upon their own ground;/ never again shall they be plucked/ From the land I have given them,/ say I, the LORD, your God."

The good Lord will tell you when you are to stand firm on the ground where He has planted you. We must walk by faith and not by sight. It doesn't matter what is happening to you now. The question is, "Do you have faith that the word you received from the Lord is truth for your life?"

God does not say "Yes" and then "No." He is consistent with His blessings for you, and He will never undo His plan for you. Moreover, He will never take back the grace He has promised you. Rejoice and be glad, for God has given you the kingdom!

I praise You, Jesus, for all eternity and give thanks for Your blessings.

Are you assured that God's perfect plan for you includes His many blessings and eternal life in heaven? Knowing that, we give thanks and praise!

Matthew 13:23 "But the seed sown on rich soil is the one who hears the word and understands it, who indeed bears fruit and yields a hundred or sixty or thirtyfold."

Do you have rich soil in your life? How do you know? The answer is in how much fruit you bear in your life. Are your daily activities a witness for the Lord? Does anyone even know you believe in Christ by listening to you?

I know it is impossible to bear a hundredfold fruit unless we totally surrender our will to the Lord. There is no doubt that Jesus wants to give us the power to spread the Gospel to bring hundreds or more into His kingdom. We just must ask God for this power and focus on His love.

Lord, use me to bear the fruit that brings a hundredfold-plus into Your kingdom.

What gifts and talents do you have to share that can be used to help bring people to God's kingdom?

Acts 2:34-35 "For David did not go up into heaven, but he himself said:/ 'The Lord said to my Lord,/ "Sit at my right hand/ until I make your enemies your footstool."'"

Who are your enemies? They might not be who you think. They are not those who work with you, your neighbors or even family members. Your enemies are the devil and the fallen angels—nothing more, nothing less. We battle them daily.

I have great news for you! Jesus has won the battle. You need not fear. The devil is a created creature. He is not God! He only exists for God's purpose—something we can't understand. We do know Jesus has given us power through His name and the Holy Spirit to make the enemy our footstool. Rejoice!

Thank You Lord for giving me victory over my enemies. I praise Your name!

Are you aware that God has given you many gifts to battle and reject evil? You must recognize what is not of God and discern when you are attacked.

2 Corinthians 7:16 "I rejoice, because I have confidence in you in every respect."

Do you think the Lord has confidence in you? Do you believe in yourself? The good news is you can have full confidence in the Lord and in what He will do through you.

Many times, I doubt myself and ask, "What I am doing with my life?" However, I realize that it's not my power that makes the difference, but the power of Jesus. Our confidence in the Lord comes from our constant trust and faith in God, and this will bring us peace. Remember, He forever holds us in the palm of His hand. And, through His redeeming love we are saved.

I rejoice in You, my Savior, and praise You for the confidence that You have given me for today and always.

Are you aware that God wants to bless you with confidence in Him and in the life you are leading?

Matthew 25:13 "Therefore, stay awake, for you know neither the day nor the hour.

I find it fascinating that many people live their life as if they will live this life forever. Guess what? We are going to be dead a lot longer than we live on this earth. As James says in his letter, "We are but a vapor that appears briefly and then disappears."

It is critical we live each day as if it was our last day. We don't know when our eternity comes. We might meet our Maker today or in 50 years. Only the Lord knows for sure.

Lord, let me focus on You and be prepared today to be with You for all eternity. praise You for being with me for all of eternity.

Why is it important to be faithful to the Lord during your short stay here on Earth? Do you realize your future in heaven depends on it.? Praise God now and you will spend eternity praising Him in heaven.

Nehemiah 2:18 "Then I explained to them how the favoring hand of my God had rested upon me...."

God's hand is upon you when you ask Him into your life! One of the biggest challenges in this world is to spend time trusting Him for our present and for our future. Indeed, Jesus clearly said not to worry about the future. However, it is very difficult to do that. We fret about finances, our relationships, our children, etc. What will happen?

I have great news! Life will be a blessing if we allow Jesus in! Life definitely won't be how *we* planned it, but it will happen in God's perfect time. Rejoice!

Lord, I praise You for having Your hand upon me.

Do you feel blessed knowing God has His hand upon you? He loves you so much, because you are His child.

Luke 5:5 "Simon said in reply, 'Master, we have worked hard all night and have caught nothing, but at your command I will lower the nets.'"

I love this story because it brings together both the reality of the world and our need to put our faith and trust in Jesus. Simon and his fellow fishermen had been fishing all night and had caught nothing. Today, if someone told you to go right back to what you had been doing, what would be your response?

Simon, soon to be named Peter, applied faith to the logic of the world and said that he "believed in Jesus more than he believed in his own instincts." The result? They gathered so many fish the nets could barely hold them. So also will it be with the blessings that flow from Jesus when we trust him.

Lord teach me to be obedient to Your will and to Your Word. I praise You for being my "coach."

Do you feel following God's will is a challenge? He is there to lead you. Do you listen to what He asks of you? Read His Scriptures and follow His laws. You will be rewarded!

Psalm 119:105 "A lamp to my feet is your word,/ a light to my path."

In this world, there are many dark corners, uncertain curves, and bumpy roads. It often appears foggy and difficult to see. However, God's Word is a light for our journey on earth. It guides us, especially when we need it the most.

When I find myself struggling with a life decision, I ask the Lord for guidance. And, when I am in my deepest period of questioning, I turn to God's Word, where I find His peace and guidance. Indeed, it lights my path and directs my journey.

Praise You, Jesus, for Your Word, a "lamp unto my feet and a light unto my path."

God our Father is the only truth we need. He guides us perfectly. Do you feel at peace and thankful? Do you believe in His love for you?

Ephesians 6:2-3 "'Honor your father and mother.' This is the first commandment with a promise, 'that it may go well with you and that you may have a long life on earth.'"

During my life, I've been amazed by just how many people ignore their parents, or even worse, have nothing to do with them. This lack of respect, according to God's own Word, will have consequences, perhaps even eternal.

If you are a parent, you know how difficult and painful parenting can be. You made mistakes. You didn't learn how to do be a parent in college. Forgive your parents! They tried their best. They weren't perfect, just as you aren't perfect. Call them today! See them before it is too late.

Lord, I praise you for the parents you gave me. Teach me to honor them in every way.

Do you honor your parents by increasing the faith they gave you? Do you honor your parents for the goodness they taught you? How do you love them?

Ephesians 6:18 "With all prayer and supplication, pray at every opportunity in the Spirit. To that end, be watchful with all perseverance and supplication for all the holy ones."

Praying in the Spirit, if you believe in the gifts of the Holy Spirit, means "praying in tongues." This is a heavenly language made manifest by the Holy Spirit praying through you to the Father for things we can't fully fathom or understand. It is very important to pray this way for the "holy ones."

Never grow discouraged with your prayer life. Jesus loves perseverance. It is critical for success in our spiritual life.

Lord, teach me how to pray without ceasing and remind me to pray for all the holy ones. I praise You for the gift of prayer.

Did you know praying in the Spirit allows you to give greater glory to God? Do you realize how powerful it is? People are healed, and lives are transformed! Thank God for this gift of prayer.

Judges 6:12 "[T]he angel of the LORD appeared to him and said, 'The LORD is with you, O champion!'"

Gideon, as mentioned in the book of Judges, was scared. Not only was he overwhelmed by the power of his oppressors and enemies, the Midianites, but he also was living in the flesh. Furthermore, he doubted the ability of God to defeat his enemies. This is similar to our own lack of faith in God to guide our life.

Then something dramatically changed. God intervened directly into the life of Gideon. God sent an angel to appear before him, telling him how the Lord saw him. God saw Gideon as the Savior of his people, if he would only trust the Lord to let His power flow through him. Although, Gideon ended up testing God, he ultimately allowed the power of God to win the day. In the same way, God's power will be victorious in our lives.

I praise you Lord for making me a champion for your people.

Do you want to bring greater glory to God's kingdom? If you allow Him to act in your life, He will use you to perform great feats.

Isaiah 25:1 "O LORD, you are my God,/ I will extol you and praise your name;/ For you have fulfilled your wonderful plans of old,/ faithful and true."

How many times in your life have you felt abandoned by God? He hasn't heard your prayers—or so you think. You want things to happen in your timing and in your will.

God is patient because He knows what is best for you. God is always faithful and true. He does not say "Yes" and then say "No." He will fulfill all His promises for you, but in His way and in His timing. For this reason, you should praise Him for all things, because it is part of the divine plan for your life and for the glory of the Lord.

I praise and thank You Lord for fulfilling the plans You have for my life.

Do you notice God working in your life? Maybe He presents His works in many small ways. Or maybe He moves mountains. Thank Him.

Hebrews 10:35-36 "Therefore, do no throw away your confidence; it will have great recompense. You need endurance to do the will of God and receive what He has promised."

In the flesh, it is easy to get discouraged and depressed. That is when the endurance of my faith must be made manifest. At times, I need to do a gut check and realize my confidence is not in myself, but in the Lord. He is the Victor and my Benefactor. Do you think David would have met Goliath without the strength of the Lord on his side? Why do you try to win without God's presence and power in your life?

Lord, I praise Your name for teaching me patience and endurance. I know You will fulfill Your promises in my life.

Do you feel the need for patience and endurance to live in the life of the Holy Spirit? Did you know living in God's perfect will means you give up control and are willing to wait for God to do His work in you and your life?

Acts 7:60 "...'Lord, do not hold this sin against them'..."

St. Steven followed in the tradition of Jesus when he forgave his killers. As he was being stoned, Steven prayed for forgiveness for those who were killing him. Would we do the same? In business, as in life, we are going to be hurt by people who do wrong to us. They might be gossiping or in the worse circumstance, slandering us.

Jesus knows how weak the human condition is and still loves us unconditionally. He even expects us to fall to our flesh, as demonstrated in his telling Peter that he would deny him three times before the cock crowed.

What should we do when those who seek us harm attack us? We need to turn to the Lord for strength.

Lord, help us forgive as Jesus and St. Steven forgave. Teach me how to forgive those who hurt me today and always. I praise You for the gift of forgiveness.

Do you understand there are only benefits when forgiving those who have harmed you? Do you realize you will receive God's grace when you forgive?

Isaiah 59:21 "My spirit is upon you/ and my words that I have put into your mouth/ Shall never leave your mouth,/ nor the mouths of your children/ Nor the mouths of your children's children/ from now on and forever, says the LORD.

If you are a parent, you probably worry. You worry about everything from how your young children will grow up, the morality of your teenagers, even the spirituality of your young adults. My parents would tell me that you never stop being a parent. I understand now what they meant.

With this verse, the Lord is comforting us. Indeed, His Spirit is upon us and His Word will not return void from our mouths. God, who is love, knows the desire of our heart is for our children to be blessed. Therefore, God desires that His Word bear fruit in our lives and is imparted to our children and children's children.

Lord, I praise and thank you for blessing my family forever!

God blesses your family when you love each other, pray together and put God first in your family life. How does your family praise God?

Proverbs 18:7 "The fool's mouth is his ruin;/ his lips are a snare to his life."

Have you ever said anything you regretted? I know I have.

Indeed, what we share in common is the tendency, at times, to speak first and think second. I know, in my life, doing so has gotten me in trouble, mostly with my family and friends, but also at work with my coworkers.

Sometimes, I have felt like a fool when I have "lived out" this verse. One of the key aspects of walking the Christian life is to control your speech. In fact, Scripture tells us we will be held accountable for every idle word we say. If we are living a life of conflict and arguments, we can be sure we are living in the flesh.

Repent and let the joy and peace of the risen Christ be with you!

Lord, help me to control my words so that they are sweet incense to You. I praise You for the fruit of self-control.

Do you find it is important to repent for the wrong things you say? It is also important to ask God to help you love His people with kind words.

Luke 5:32 "I have not come to call the righteous to repentance but sinners."

I don't know about you, but this verse is very comforting to me.

I have felt, at times, like the biggest sinner in the world. Regardless, the one thing I am certain of is that I need a savior.

There is one major difference between Christianity and other faiths. Essentially, all other religions are based on the individual working his or her way into heaven. Through Christ, we realize there is only one way to salvation. We are saved through the grace of God and the blood of Jesus.

Lord, I praise and thank You for dying on the cross and for Your saving grace.

Do you focus on God's great gift of Jesus and His love for you? Do you fully understand Jesus' gift of love and His dying to save all of God's people?

Proverbs 22:9 "The kindly man will be blessed,/ for he gives his sustenance to the poor."

To be blessed is to be in the state of grace. It is something God desires for all of us. One way to be blessed is to take care of the poor. The question is what does that mean for your life? Will writing an occasional check for an anti-poverty agency do it?

The most important thing is to have a heart of compassion for those who need of love. We immediately think only material things are necessary for the poor. However, I believe their most essential need is to feel loved and to help them in whatever way is required. It could be accomplished through kind words or helping them to learn new skills and/or finding work. Perhaps, it is simply to visit the lonely. Regardless, the kindly man is prepared to do it.

Help me Lord, to live a life as a kindly person. I praise You for this grace.

Do you struggle to love all God's people? You are not alone.

Corinthians 11:14-15 "And no wonder, for even Satan masquerades as an angel of light. So it is not strange that his ministers also masquerade as ministers of righteousness. Their end will correspond to their deeds."

In life, one of the most important decisions to make is knowing whom to trust. If you are in a position of influence or power, it is common to have individuals flatter you and try to benefit from their association with you.

Beware! Some of these people will turn on you quickly if it suits their interests. You might think they are your friends—clearly, they are not! It is best to look at the character and heart of the people you entrust with your interests.

Lord, give me Your wisdom to associate with those who uphold Your truth. I praise You for being my strength and my shield.

Do you surround yourself with those who fear God? They will influence you to be Christ-like and help build the kingdom of God with you.

2 Corinthians 6:14 "Do not be yoked with those who are different, with unbelievers. For what partnership do righteousness and lawlessness have? Or what fellowship does light have with darkness?"

I believe this verse is a cornerstone for success in life. Obviously, to take a spouse who is not a believer is a huge risk. It is something I definitely wouldn't recommend, based on this Scripture. One of the best decisions I've made is to yoke myself with believers—men and women who share my values and integrity.

Lord, may I always yoke myself with believers. I praise You for sending them in my life.

Have you ever tried being with someone who doesn't believe in God? How has the experience been difficult? Compare that with being with believers.

Philippians 2:14 "Do everything without grumbling or questioning.

Can you imagine what kind of world this would be if people never grumbled? I almost couldn't even fathom what it would be like. Try sometimes to go a whole day without grumbling at all.

I know God blesses us when we are positive about life, praise Him for all things and never complain. That is the Christian attitude we are to have each and every day.

When Jesus speaks of our being the light of the world, this is primarily what He means. To love is to have a smile on our faces and never grumble about things not being perfect.

Jesus, help me to live a life full of love and less grumbling. I praise You for the gift of a "heavenly attitude."

Are you aware when you grumble and are negative about your life, you are not living in God's perfect will? He wants you to be happy. Do you praise Him for all things in your life? Do you see how God might be working in your life when you are given difficulties?

Philippians 2:8 "[H]e humbled himself,/ becoming obedient to death,/ even death on a cross."

To be humble of heart is a key to the heart of God. And, to love unconditionally and put other's needs first before our own is to do God's will. That is exactly what Jesus did for us. He most certainly demonstrated humility in allowing Himself to die on the cross for our sins.

Many times, we may feel badly about the lack of respect we get from others. We might feel slighted. When that happens, think of Jesus. We have been mistreated. Not respected? Abused? Who are we to complain?

Thank You Jesus for teaching me how to be humble of heart. I praise You for the gift of humility.

Do you realize that Jesus didn't grumble when He paid the ultimate price? Does Jesus' act of humility put things in perspective for you?

1 Peter 3:9 "Do not return evil for evil, or insult for insult; but, on the contrary, a blessing, because to this you were called, that you might inherit a blessing."

In my life, I've had to fight the urge to get revenge on those who have hurt me. The revenge might be an insult, an unkind word or even worse. All of this is of the flesh.

Jesus wants us to turn the other cheek. He asks us to return love for insult. We are to love unconditionally, even if it doesn't come back in any way. When we do this, Jesus gives us eternal blessings. This is the will of the Father.

Lord Jesus, give us the strength not to return evil for evil, but to bless those who harm us. I praise You for Your strength.

Do you realize that living in the Spirit requires you to resist the temptation to hurt those who have injured you in any way? Love them with the love of the Father!

1 Thessalonians 4:3 "This is the will of the God, your holiness: that you refrain from immorality."

Immorality can manifest itself in many ways. Obviously, the most common is sexual. However, immorality is also dishonesty in dealing with others.

Another common way immortality manifests itself is through speech. Often it is seen through dirty jokes. What do you do when someone says something off-color or gossips? Do you say nothing? Or do you try to tell that person how you feel about it, thereby spreading the light of Jesus? It is hard, but that is what we are to do!

Lord, teach me how to be moral in all things and at all times. I praise You for Your strength in this area of my life.

Are you bold and live the life God wants for you? Do you stand up for what is right? You may be persecuted, but the Father will be pleased with you.

Isaiah 1:19 "If you are willing, and obey,/ you shall eat the good things of the land."

Obedience to the Lord is one of the most critical aspects of the Christian walk. It is tempting to venture into the "world of gray" when we interface with the world of the flesh. That world tells us the ends justifies the means; do whatever it takes to get what you want.

We are the light of the world and the light of Jesus when we follow His commandments. Yes, we may lose some friends along the way if we follow the Lord's way. However, the blessings that will come to us when we are obedient will be beyond our comprehension—for this world and the next.

Lord, teach me never to compromise my values in the pursuit of success. I praise You for being my teacher.

Isn't it better to reap the rewards of the Father rather than sin against Him?

Proverbs 15:29 "The LORD is far from the wicked,/ but the prayer of the just he hears."

If you are like most of us, you sometimes wonder if the Lord hears your prayers. Perhaps they are not being answered in the way we think they should. We pray and pray, and nothing seems to be happening.

Know that when you are a child of God, your prayers are being heard. God believes in you and wants to bless you abundantly. However, He will grant your prayer requests in accordance with His will and what is best for your spiritual growth and eternal blessings. Trust Him for He always hears your prayers and will always respond in a loving way.

Lord, I trust in You and know that You will grant my prayer requests in accordance to Your perfect will.

Do you sometimes think you know what is better for you than God? Do you realize the Father knows what is best for your spirit? He is saving you from yourself. Praise Him.

Luke 18:1 "He told them a parable about the necessity for them to pray always without becoming weary."

The longer I walk in the Lord, the more I realize the importance of prayer and the critical practice of praying without ceasing. The essential aspect of prayer is perseverance. The Lord is asking, "Do you love Me?"

The more we pray, the more we enter into the presence of the Lord. I believe God does not always answer our prayers quickly; He is teaching us patience and desires us to remain in Him as He remains in us. Do not despair or lose heart, because God's joyous plan is unfolding in our life.

Lord Jesus, I praise You and rejoice in Your plan that is unfolding in my life.

Do you pray for patience as you await God's revelation and plan for your life? The more you pray, the closer you are to Him and to understanding His way.

Nahum 1:7 "The LORD is good,/ a refuge on the day of distress;/ He takes care of those who have recourse to him."

All of us have days when we feel like giving up. Things are not going well. What we thought was going to happen, didn't. Perhaps we are not getting along with our spouse, kids, friends or co-workers.

The temptation is to retreat and be alone. However, God desires for us always to be in community. This community starts with God and our communicating together in prayer. He often brings people into our lives who bless and comfort us with words from the Lord. Remember the Lord's words: "Do not fear, for I am with you."

Rejoice, for I am with you, says the Lord. I praise and thank You Jesus!

Knowing that God is beside us at all times is an amazing revelation. Do you believe this is reality for you?

Deuteronomy 8:18 "Remember then, it is the LORD, your God, who gives you the power to acquire wealth, by fulfilling, as he has now done, the covenant which he swore to your fathers."

How much do you rely on your own talent to be successful? Do you think it is your own intelligence, initiative, creativity and overall skills that bring you success with relationships, jobs, business or life in general? It is easy to think that way. Often, we have relied on our experience and ourselves in the past. When we get in trouble, we then decide to pray and turn to God.

This verse and others make it very clear. We need to do our best at work, being mindful that everything in our lives that bears good fruit comes from the grace of God. Remember the old saying: "God helps those who help themselves?" There is some truth to that, but God also helps those who simply turn to Him in love and faith.

Lord, I praise You for any success You have given me and will give me. I love You!

Do you owe all your life to God? Do you see Him not only as Creator but Director in your life? Praise Him!

Psalm 55:23 "Cast your care upon the Lord, and he will support you; never will he permit the just man to be disturbed."

One of the best sayings I've heard is, "No one can outdo God's generosity." I feel a big part of life is trusting in God. It is turning to Him in good times and bad. It means the faith you put in Jesus will always bring blessings to your life.

If you are right with God, He will give you the fruits of the spirit. You will never be concerned about your future because you know that He will take care of you and your family. You will be filled with His peace, joy and love.

Jesus, I praise You and rejoice in You for taking care of my troubles and being with me always.

God wants to protect you from harm and any troubles in your life. Do you rely on Him? Do you pray, asking for His help?

1 Corinthians 14:33 "God is a God, not of confusion, but of peace."

If there is confusion in your life, then something is not right in your relationship with the Lord. He is not a God who holds anything back. He gives you His voice and His will—and shows you how to handle your life.

Does that mean He tells us what job to take, vacation to go on or food to eat? Not necessarily. It means that anything truly important to your salvation and faith will be made evident. Much of the rest of your life does not matter in terms of what God desires. He will bless it when we turn it over to Him.

Lord, I praise and thank You for giving me the grace to know Your will in all things that are truly important.

When there is confusion in your life and with the choices you are making, do you feel God is interceding, asking you to question your decisions and look to Him for guidance? Do you quiet your heart and become open to His will?

Hebrews 13:6 "Thus we say with confidence:/ 'The Lord is my helper,/[and] I will not be afraid./ What can anyone do to me?'"

This is another critical verse to memorize, especially in stressful life situations. How many times do we quake in fear in anticipation of a meeting that we deem very important? It might be an important conversation with someone you are close to or care about. I have seen many people spend sleepless nights and even get physically sick with worry.

I have often thought about how Jesus felt, standing before Pilate. Yes, He is God, but also human. I'm sure there were moments of anguish. However, Jesus knew the only power Pilate possessed was power given to Him by the Father. Jesus did not fear! Why should we? Always remember, that the intent of our Lord is to bless and protect us from harm. Jesus knows our future, so rejoice and be glad!

I praise and thank You, Lord, for being my helper and for staying by my side, no matter what.

Do you often need help in your stressful interactions? Call on Jesus for His help in any circumstance.

2 Kings 6:16-17 "'Do not be afraid,' Elisha answered, 'Our side outnumbers theirs.' Then he prayed, 'O LORD, open his eyes, that he might see.'"

The king of Aram wanted to kill Elisha because the prophet was aiding the king of Israel. The king sent a strong army to complete the task, with great confidence of its success.

Fear would have been the natural response when seeing this mighty army. And that is exactly what happened to Elisha's attendant. However, Elisha, as a man of God, knew differently. He prayed his attendant would see the truth. Indeed, the attendant's eyes were opened, and he saw a mountain filled with chariots that would protect them.

The storms in our lives that hit us appear to be sinking us, but rejoice! God is with you!

Lord, open my eyes to see Your truth and protection. I praise You now and forever.

God doesn't want you to feel despair. Do you let Him into your heart and feel His love? Letting Jesus into your heart, you will feel confident and ready to face difficult trials.

2 Timothy 2:21 "If anyone cleanses himself of these things, he will be a vessel for lofty use, dedicated, beneficial to the master of the house, ready for every good work."

Paul warns us to avoid evil at all cost. If we allow evil to enter our lives, we are profaned and can't be used by our Master.

However, when we repent and avoid all evil, we are blessed and used by Jesus to build the kingdom. It was for this reason we have been created—to be used as a vessel for good works. It is not to collect material things, but spiritual gifts to build the kingdom.

Lord, I praise and thank You for purifying me so that I will be ready for every good work.

Do you ask the Lord to purify your heart? Do you realize this purification allows you to do His work?

Timothy 6:17 "Tell the rich in the present age not to be proud and not to rely on so uncertain a thing as wealth but rather on God, who richly provides us with all things for our enjoyment."

Perhaps you should read this again. Think about how you spend your time and for what reason. What are your goals? Are they for this life or beyond? Is your kingdom on this earth or in heaven?

If you are honest with yourself, you might admit the pursuit of wealth and material things often drives your daily activities. Many of us believe, through the lies of the world, that more money means more happiness for our families and ourselves.

Don't we want the bigger house and car? That is what the world wants you to believe. But nothing could be further from the truth. Jesus is the only source of happiness and contentment we'll find in this world or the next. It is He provides our peace and joy on earth.

Jesus, may I always know the truth of what is important in my life. I praise You for being my way, truth, and life!

Do you see the blessings in your life are eternal?

Psalm 48:15 "[T]hat such is God,/ Our God forever and ever;/ he will guide us."

Often, we wander through life in confusion. We fret over what job to take, stock to buy, church to attend or whom to marry.

We worry when we don't get a sign of God's presence and direction. The good news is that it really doesn't matter what we do, if we first proclaim it in the name of the Lord. When we put God at the center of our activity, it will be blessed.

God's guidance comes from His own authority, through the power of the Holy Spirit. When we trust Him, He will guide us to Himself every time and ultimately to His kingdom in heaven.

Believe it! It's true!

Lord, I praise Your name for guiding me into Your heavenly kingdom.

Do you realize all you need is God's grace to guide you through life? If you follow Him, you will have everlasting life. Are you ready to choose Him and His ways so everything else falls into place?

Luke 11:41 "But as to what is within, give alms, and behold, everything will be clean for you."

We are all sinners; we all fall short of the mark. That is why we need God's grace and the blood of His son Jesus to save us. We know from Scripture that love will cover a multitude of sins. However, many of us may not be aware that giving alms to the poor also makes us clean before Him; if we trust God we will be blessed because we are providing for His people.

Lord, I praise You for teaching me how to use my finances to build the kingdom of God.

Did you know, as a Christian, you have been charged with a responsibility to care for God's people? If you see people asking for help, and you assist them with money or the necessities of life, God will bless you with His Grace. Are you aware that you glorify God when you care for all His people, and you "live the Gospel" when you perform acts of charity?

Matthew 26:42 "Withdrawing a second time, he prayed again, 'My Father, if it is not possible that this cup pass without my drinking it, your will be done!'"

The agony of Jesus in Gethsemane is something we will never know. However, all of us experience those dark moments of despair, when nothing seems to be right. Do we simply ask God to take it away?

Jesus, once again, provided the perfect example of humility. He knew the most important thing was not the pain, suffering or personal feelings, but doing the will of the Father.

We are here on earth, I believe, to build the kingdom of the Father, "on earth as it is in heaven." How do we do this? Once again, Jesus gives us the "how to." Simply to surrender our will to His. When we do this, we become more like Him and allow others to relish in His love and light.

Lord, may Your will be done in my life today and every day. I praise You for being my support and my life.

Do want to live in God's Perfect will? You will be greatly rewarded, and you will receive His grace.

Exodus 15:26 "'If you really listen to the voice of the LORD, your God...and do what is right in his eyes: if you heed his commandments and keep all his precepts, I will not afflict with any of the diseases with which I afflicted the Egyptians; for I, the LORD, am your Healer."

What areas in your life need healing? My guess is, if you are like the rest of us, a lot more than you think. Most of us have little idea of what is going on with us physically, mentally or spiritually. Would you even know if you had a major disease? I've known many people who didn't find out until they had weeks to live.

We need God as our healer in every area of our life. He will heal us physically, but more importantly, spiritually. He will heal those sinful patterns in our life, if we let Him. Jesus came so that we may have peace, joy, love and an abundant life.

Help me, Lord. I praise You for healing me in every way possible so that I may better serve Your kingdom.

Our Lord wants to heal every aspect of your life. Will you let Him heal you through His Holy Spirit?

Matthew 19:26 "For human beings this is impossible, but for God all things are possible."

When we hear that "for God and with God "all things are possible, what does that mean? Is it conditional? Is it seasonal? Does it depend on our behavior?

It is amazing how most of us discount what our Creator can do in our lives. We have a tough time on our job? Perhaps, we think, God doesn't care or can't change anything. Do our actions often say our sickness is beyond the healing power of our Lord Jesus? Are we having a difficult time with family? Yes, Jesus does care and He will heal and bless us, if only we have the faith of a tiny mustard seed.

Lord, increase my faith so that I may realize that with You all things are possible. I praise You for the gift of faith.

Did you know anything is possible with God? Faith the size of a tiny mustard seed is all He needs to sow, cultivate and nurture us into a more mature spiritual life.

Proverbs 26:28 "The lying tongue is its owner's enemy,/ and the flattering mouth works ruin."

God hates lying as much as any other sin. Why? If you lie, you are incapable of loving at the moment of the lie. Also, the lie can do incredible damage. Many people lie for personal gain. Individuals who flatter are nearly as bad as liars. They probably don't fully believe the wonderful things they are saying about you. In fact, many times, they may say the opposite behind your back.

The most important thing for our behavior is not to respond in kind. We must love others unconditionally, but we don't have to receive their lies or flattering messages. We need to stick to the truth about life and the message of Jesus.

Lord Jesus, protect us against liars and those who seek to harm us. I praise You for my protection.

When people lie to you, you may not even be aware of the harm caused. Do you pray for people you meet and for conversations filled with truth?

Proverbs 25:21-22 "If your enemy be hungry, give him food to eat,/ if he be thirsty, give him to drink; For live coals you will heap on his head,/ and the LORD will vindicate you."

Being a faith-filled Christian is opposite of how the world behaves. Christians must love everyone, even their enemies. Who in the world would treat an enemy kindly? When you love unconditionally and don't respond in kind to the evil of your enemy, God will lift you up on high.

Your enemies won't know what to do when you fail to respond negatively. They will be anxious because they won't know how to act. However, God knows how to act. He will heap blessings upon you.

Lord, give me the courage to love my enemies. I praise You for the gift of forgiveness.

Are you positive around your enemies? Do you try to be compassionate and to understand where they are coming from? Actually, they are sharing their burdens and troubles when they attack you with their harmful words. Do you pray for them and forgive them?

Proverbs 10:30 "The just man will never be disturbed,/ but the wicked will not abide in the land."

How comforting it is that the just man is never disturbed! We can trust God for all things in our life. We do not have to fear or wonder if we are alone; we are never alone when we have God with us in faith.

The wicked have no power over you. When you are being slandered or mistreated, do not worry for God will protect you. Go forth and spread the Gospel of the Lord. The evil about you will never enter your house.

I praise and thank You, Jesus, for protecting me from attack.

Do you pray for God's protection when under attack? Do you ask the Father to protect you from harm with Jesus' precious blood, with the power of the Holy Spirit and through the intercession of your Blessed Mother?

Colossians 1:25 "...I am a minister in accordance with God's stewardship given to me to bring to completion for you the word of God."

We are called to be stewards for the Lord. For me, it means giving all my time, talent and treasure to the Lord. Many people focus on tithing 10% of their income to the Lord. That is a very good thing, but I believe, it misses the point. We need to give 100% of our money, our time and all the gifts he has given us—back to Him. When we do that, we are blessed with even more graces!

If we do not spread the gospel, then who will? We're here on earth to build the kingdom; we are to spread the Word on earth, as it is in heaven; that is, to complete what Jesus has started for us.

I praise You for giving me the gift of being an evangelist.

Do you understand that when you use all your gifts to be an evangelist, the Father will bless you? You will be doing His work in your life. Do you know that you will receive joy "all the days of your life" and then, delight in the joy of heaven?

Acts 9:4 "He fell to the ground and heard a voice saying to him, 'Saul, Saul, why are you persecuting me?'"

Sometimes God must get our attention in a big way. He will knock us off our horse to get us to realize that He is God. Paul's sin, and our sin, is in persecuting Jesus and His people. It causes division and discord.

We, like Saul, need to repent. We need to make a complete change in our life, a "metanoia" to help build up God's kingdom. Saul was working for the devil without realizing it. We must be careful we aren't doing the same. Ask Jesus to have the Holy Spirit reveal the truth for our life.

One of the biggest blessings in my life is my son-in-law. Today is his birthday. He is filled with the Spirit, a man of God. He is the answer to many prayers. When our daughter was growing up, we prayed she would marry a spirit-filled husband. Praise God!

Come Lord Jesus, mold me into Your image so that I may do your will in building Your church. I praise You now and forever.

Do you accept the Father's perfect will so that your life will be filled with action on His behalf?

Proverbs 13:22 "The good man leaves an inheritance to his children's children,/ but the wealth of the sinner is stored up for the just."

Today is the celebration of my father's birthday. We had a party for him on his 90th birthday, with 85 friends and family present. We were all very blessed to have my father in our lives. His life was devoted to his family, and he worked hard so we could be successful in our lives. However, he taught us God was first, family second and the job a distant last. He also stressed, "to enjoy what you have and not be envious of others." He always said his backyard was "Switzerland." That is the inheritance he gave his family.

My father would often say, "There are no pockets in coffins," and "If you have your health, you are a millionaire." This is far greater than any inheritance of wealth.

Lord, I praise and thank You for my father. Bless him, forever, in heaven.

Do you believe God is the Father of all fathers? May the fathers in your life be filled with God's guidance.

1 Thessalonians 5:9 "For God did not destine us for wrath, but to gain salvation through our Lord Jesus Christ."

If things are not going well in your life, rejoice God is with you! He has not destined us for despair or to live a life of suffering. Jesus told us we would have a life of abundance. That abundance begins when we give our lives to Jesus. Then we begin to experience joy and peace in our life.

There are days we feel nothing is going right. Maybe today is a day like that. If it is, know that great things are in store for you. Jesus wants to bless you with all the spiritual blessings in the heaven.

Come Lord Jesus, and fill me with Your Holy Spirit today and every day. I praise You for Your love and for answering my prayers according to Your perfect will!

Open your heart to the Holy Spirit. Welcome the power, the grace and the love of the Lord into your heart. When you do this, anything is possible. You will have all you need to fulfill His perfect will.

Jude 1:20 "But you, beloved build your selves up in your most holy faith; pray in the Holy Spirit."

Each day, our goal should be how to build ourselves up in the Lord. It is something that God wants to do for us. His desire is to bless us at all times.

I believe in the gifts of the Holy Spirit. I know Jesus wants us to do what He did and even more. In that case, "praying in the Spirit" gives us the power to do the things Jesus has created for us. All we need to do is say "Yes" to Jesus. Then, allow the Holy Spirit to enter our lives and pray in the spirit with all of His power and for His glory.

Come, Holy Spirit, fill me with Your presence. I praise You for leading me to Jesus and for being my Advocate.

Do you believe gifts of the Holy Spirit are so powerful? When you use those gifts in Jesus' name, great power and glory are released onto those you pray for. Do you experience great healing in your life and the lives of others?

Proverbs 20:21 "Possessions gained hastily at the outset/ will in the end not be blessed."

When we begin a new job or project, we usually want to be successful quickly. However, that might not be the best course of action. God wants us to turn our work over to Him. Often, that means that He will teach us patience, so that we rely on only Him.

It is in our best interest to be successful in the Lord's timing. If we rush it, we will be on our own and will not receive the power God desires us to have in our work.

Lord, may I desire Your success in Your time. I praise You for strength and wisdom.

When things come too easily in your life, your spirit has difficulty growing in patience. Challenges and sufferings in life allow you to come to Jesus for His help. In turn, your spiritual life becomes strong and full of wisdom. Are you open to this time of living?

1 Peter 4:2 "...[S]o as not to spend what remains of one's life in the flesh on human desires, but on the will of God."

It is very critical that we pray for God's will in our lives. There is a reason why the Lord's Prayer mentions "Thy will be done." He wants us to ask through the Holy Spirit, and then He will act.

We need to test ourselves on whether our flesh is dictating our actions. How do we spend our time? What are our thoughts? Does our life bear good fruit for the Lord?

Lord, help me only to desire Your will in my life. I love and praise Your holy name.

It isn't easy choosing God's will in your life. Doesn't it mean you must sacrifice your wants of the flesh? The immediate concerns in the physical world can be powerful. Do you pray for the grace of God to aid you at all times? This will create a desire of wanting only His will.

John 20:29 "...'Have you come to believe because you have seen me? Blessed are those who have not seen and have believed."

In our life journey, we are often called to believe when we have no evidence or proof for that belief. Perhaps it is a health issue or a relationship.

How often do we believe only after the obvious has occurred? We are told something good is about to happen or that we will be getting it soon. When things don't turn out as we had expected, we lose faith again. It is critical to stand firm!

Even if you don't understand what God is doing in your life, can you focus on your trust and faith in the Lord to pull you through those times of doubt? Rely on the fact that God will reveal the reason for His will in your life.

Help me, Lord, have faith when I don't see the result I want. I praise You for the gift of faith!

Do you feel the gift of faith is critical in all aspects of your life? Does it help you appreciate all of God's works in your life?

November 24

Luke 24: 53 "...[A]nd they were continually in the temple praising God."

While living the life of Christ, we should reflect on what the disciples did to gain access to the presence of God. One of the most important aspects of their spirituality was gathering together daily and praying as a community. However, it was more than just praying; they praised God with all their hearts, souls and might. You might ask yourself, "How can I constantly be praising God? " Simply, this can be done by having an attitude of prayer at work and by praising God for each personal interaction and action you take. Then you are praising Him "in all things."

Lord, may I praise You with every breath that I have today.

Do you experience deep prayer? Reflecting on God's love will aid you in praising God all the time. When has the true presence of God the Father infused and permeated your heart? Were you filled with overflowing joy? It is overwhelming when it happens!

Luke 19:8 "But Zacchaeus stood there and said to the Lord, 'Behold, half my possessions, Lord, I shall give to the poor, and if I have extorted anything from anyone, I shall repay it four times over.'"

Why was Jesus extremely pleased with this rich tax collector named Zacchaeus? Jesus told His disciples salvation had come to the house of this tax collector and that He was a descendent of Abraham. I believe the grace in Zacchaeus allowed his faith in Jesus to be stronger than his belief in material wealth. Unlike the rich man in another story, Zacchaeus was prepared to give up his wealth for the Lord. He did not make wealth his God.

We have heard the saying that love of money is the root of all evil. What makes material lust so bad is that it takes over our souls and spirits. If you are wealthy, praise God, but know in whom your faith dwells.

Jesus, may my attitude toward wealth be the same as that of Zacchaeus. I praise You for the gifts You have and will always give me.

Do you use your resources in the physical world to bring good deeds to God's people and, in turn, bring you great blessings of joy, hope and love?

Galatians 3:9 "Consequently, those that have faith are blessed along with Abraham who had faith."

Today, I reflect on the difficulties and challenges of my life. If things aren't going well, it's because I'm using my plan, not God's.

What will make the difference with my ministry and my life? Definitely not my plan! I believe it is faith in God, who is the author of all grace. And, it is grace that makes us heirs to the throne.

Lord, give me the grace of faith that all things will work for my good when I follow Your will. I praise You for Your grace.

Praying for more faith and strength will allow God to work in you; then your works will bear good fruit for His kingdom. How often do you do that? Daily?

Isaiah 40:11 "Like a shepherd he feeds his flock;/ in his arms he gathers the lambs,/ Carrying them in his bosom,/ and leading the eves with care.

I wish that I could fully relate to this passage, but it is difficult because of our culture and the reality that I have never spent time with shepherds. However, when I have observed shepherds on trips, I have noticed several things. First, the shepherd never takes his eyes off his flock. He constantly watches and make sure they are safe. Second, the lambs know their shepherd's voice. They are one with it, trusting it completely. Through this trust, they are led to green pastures.

If we are still, we will hear His voice. Jesus, then, becomes our Good Shepherd. He will tend to us and lead us into His heavenly kingdom.

Lord, I praise and thank You for Your tender care and for being my Good Shepherd.

Does knowing that God is always watching you and guiding you in the right direction feel like a true blessing? Do you know, that when you stray, no matter for what reason or at what time, He will find you and welcome you back into His loving arms?

Ephesians 5:19-20 "...addressing one another [in] psalms, hymns, and spiritual songs, singing and playing to the Lord in your hearts, giving thanks always and for everything in the name of our Lord Jesus Christ to God the Father."

I love Thanksgiving. It is a day to count blessings. How many blessings do we have? I believe that "as many as there are stars in the sky" are the blessings that God has given our families. Why? Because, He loves us that much!

We can never repay God for His generosity. He has blessed us in countless ways. Some blessings we simply don't recognize or comprehend. Or, perhaps, we refuse to acknowledge them. Because God is our Creator and Redeemer, and shares with us His infinite love, generous blessings and faithfulness, we must give Him thanks and praise for all things.

Lord Jesus, I give You thanks and praise for Your unending generosity in my life.

Like your earthly father, God your Father wants to provide you with everything. Do you experience God's kindness and generosity as immeasurable and beyond your imagination?

Psalm 115:11 "Those who fear the LORD trust in the LORD;/ he is their help and their shield."

"Fearing the Lord" differs from the emotion of fear. With emotional fear, we feel anxious and out of control. However, when we fear God, we trust and acknowledge Him as our Supreme Being, our Creator. We know that God, our Good Shepherd, will take care of us for all of eternity.

Indeed, fear of the Lord is where true wisdom begins.
Fear of the Lord will guide us in finding the right priorities in our lives. Moreover, this type of "fear," along with the Word of the Lord, will be a "lamp unto our feet."

Lord, teach me to fear You in the way You deserve. I love and praise You.

Do you believe trusting in the Lord's ways allows you to fear Him and His awesome plans without faltering? Always keeping your heart on the Father will bring you countless blessings.

Titus 3:2 "They are to slander no one, to be peaceable, considerate, exercising all graciousness toward everyone."

One time when I was visiting Minnesota, I noticed something quite interesting. I'd only been there twice, but noticed the people have a unique culture. Apparently, there is an attitude called, "Minnesota nice."

Minnesotans treat each other with a great deal of courtesy and respect. Wow! Shouldn't that be the attitude of all Christians?

Wherever we go, all should see our kindness, generosity and good will. We must be careful not to slander, gossip or condemn, as is often seen in the world.

Lord, teach me to be gracious and kind toward all people. I praise You for Your kindness to me.

Are you being kind and gracious toward all of God's children? When you are, you show God's love for them? And through these actions, do you give praise to your Father and celebrate your love for Him?

December 1

Job 42:15 "In all the land, no other women were as beautiful as the daughters of Job; and their father gave them an inheritance among their brethren."

Today is my daughter's birthday. She is the jewel of my heart. I believe she is the most beautiful daughter in the world; her beauty shows both inside and outside. She is deeply devoted to both her husband and her two delightful children, and always wants to do the right thing for everyone.

I can understand why Job would give his blessing, in addition to material wealth, as an inheritance to his daughters. Job knew his daughters—like my daughter—were the foundations of life and family. And, that they would continue the inheritance of family blessings.

Lord Jesus, I praise You for giving me such a wonderful daughter.

Maybe you are someone's daughter or have a daughter yourself. Is there a person in your life who exemplifies the life-giving foundation of Jesus Christ? Reflect on that person. Do you love them for their goodness? Pray a special intention for that daughter of God.

December 2

Acts 15:35 "...Paul and Barnabas remained in Antioch, teaching and proclaiming with many others the word of the Lord."

I often think about the type of person Barnabas must have been. He was generous, adventurous and full of love, called "beloved" in Scripture and was both "helper and soul mate" to Paul. I want be a Barnabas for my community—to serve and proclaim the Word of God.

One important aspect of every vocation or job is finding balance. I recently spoke to several friends who rarely see their families because of their work. This is almost never the Lord's will. A job is not a calling; it is a career.

In having balance, we are all called to minister to God's people through service, evangelization and teaching. When we do that, we discover the joy of the Lord, find balance with our families and be at peace.

Lord, help me to find balance by being a "Barnabas" to those in my community, workplace and family. I praise You for the gift of encouragement.

In your life, do you find both little and big ways to be a "Barnabas" to someone else? Is there someone in your life that is your Barnabas? Thank God for them.

Acts 21:13 "...'I am prepared not only to be bound but even to die in Jerusalem for the name of the Lord Jesus.'"

Paul was asked by the disciples in Caesarea not to go to Jerusalem because of a prophecy that he would be bound by the Jews and given over to the Gentiles. Instead of putting himself first, Paul immediately realized that he was being tested. Did he love the Lord Jesus more than his own safety or even his life? The answer was an unqualified yes!

What would our answer be to a similar question? How much would we sacrifice for the Lord? We should ask ourselves this question every day. It will determine our priorities. Jesus won't give us more than we can handle if we trust Him.

Lord, may I do anything You ask of me, regardless of cost. Grant me Your strength. I praise You for your gift of strength.

Have you decided to entrust your life to God? Are you answering His call to sacrifice? He will give you the strength you need.

Deuteronomy 28:8 "The LORD will affirm his blessing upon you, on your barns and on all your undertakings, blessing you in the land that the LORD, your God, gives you."

We are blessed when we accept who we are in the Lord—His children! In doing so, we open the floodgate of blessings to our family and ourselves. He wants so much to give us His grace, but first we must ask for it.

Our daily activities tend to block our relationship with Jesus unless we focus on Him. When we act as if this world is our eternity, it doesn't allow room for growth in the Lord.

Lord, open my eyes to see the truth of what You have in store for me when I accept Your blessings in my life. I praise You for my blessings.

Are you open to Jesus' love during your day? Do you find Him in the gestures of kind people and then do you proclaim the Gospel by living it in your daily life? Your blessings will be immeasurable.

Ephesians 1:7 "In him we have redemption by his blood, the forgiveness of transgressions, in accord with the riches of his grace."

Today is my birthday. I don't look forward to my birthdays a great deal. The age issue is only part of it. I believe it is the reflection on all the things I would have liked to have done differently.

When I get in this mode and stay in it, I know I am not in the Lord's will. His will is that I praise Him for His eternal birthday gift, my salvation. The wonderful news I need to reflect on is His redemption, forgiveness and the grace that follows. Keep in mind the words of Blessed Teresa of Calcutta, "God has not called me to be successful but to be faithful!"

Lord, thank You for Your eternal birthday present! I praise You for the gift of eternal life.

Do you know that you are blessed to be a child of God? Do you celebrate your life and your part of God's glory? He created you for a special purpose. Reflect on what He is calling you to do in your life.

2 Timothy 1:7 "For God did not give us a spirit of cowardice but rather of power and love and self-control."

As a Christian, living in this world is not for the fainthearted. Jesus has not given us a spirit of fear or of timidity, but one of power. He has given us the grace to use self-control and not be in the flesh. How do we activate this power in our lives? The first critical step is in believing we have it.

Most Christians live fearfully of the future or what might happen to them if they live out their faith. We all struggle in this area. However, when we trust Jesus and believe that, through Him, all things will work for our good, we can step out in faith and power. Also, when we ask to His love to flow through us, we will never be disappointed!

Lord Jesus, I praise You for the spirit of power, love and self-control in my life so that I may better serve You and Your people.

The Lord is your strength. Do you look to Him for help and support when trying to be more Christ-like? In what areas would you like God's help?

1 Timothy 2:1-2 "First of all, then, I ask that supplications, prayers, petitions, and thanksgivings be offered for everyone, for kings and for all in authority, that we may lead tranquil life in all devotion and dignity."

How many of you offer supplications, prayers, petitions and, most of all, thanksgiving for the difficult people in your life—perhaps an unpleasant relative or boss? Like most people, you probably aren't sure you even want to think about them!

Amazing things happens when you pray that blessings be given to those who cause you difficulty. I have found my attitude changes immediately toward them. Gone are my negative attitude or bad feelings about them or what they may have or may not have done to me. Now I am able to be a light for the world.

Thank You Jesus for all those in authority over me. Bless them abundantly today. I praise You for putting these people in my life.

Are you aware that without Jesus as a role model, you couldn't know how to love those who exercise a difficult authority over you? Do you realize Jesus dealt with authorities in the human world? Though He showed them the truth and light, they did not always receive it.

1 Timothy 2:4 "[God] wills everyone to be saved and to come to knowledge of the truth."

It is reassuring to know God desires my salvation for all of eternity. That means that I must choose *not* to be saved—choosing, rather, to spend eternity away from His love, grace and redemption.

Why would anyone choose that? Who knows? Perhaps rebellion? Perhaps pride? Regardless, it is not for my family or me!

As for me and my household, we chose to spend eternity with our Lord Jesus in heaven!

How good is our God! Do you know He wants you to be full of His love and knowledge in eternity? He hopes you want that, too

I praise Your name for wanting to save me for all of eternity and for giving our family the gift of salvation.

Are you aware that being close to God in your heart, you will gain the knowledge to achieve everlasting life with Him?

Psalm 142:3 "My compliant I pour out before him;/ before him I lay bare my distress."

Honesty before the Lord is a very good thing. To me that means being truly candid about how I am feeling and not hiding what is happening in my life from myself and my God.

We spend much of our lives trying to please or impress each other. We are not honest about what we really feel and what our problems are. We stuff our feelings with food, alcohol and/or addictions. God wants us to complain to Him, rather than being phony about how we are really feeling. Then the Lord can begin the healing process.

Lord, give me grace always to be honest with You about how I feel.

I praise You for Your grace, now and forever!

The Lord knows what is in your heart. Do you know He wants you to trust Him enough to express all your heartaches and problems? Do you realize He wants to heal you? Do you acknowledge what needs to be healed by Him?

1 Corinthians 5:13 "God will judge those outside. 'Purge the evil person in your midst.'"

On four occasions, including three in Deuteronomy, Scripture decrees that we are to "remove evil from our midst." Why? Because we are weak and often too willing to follow and be influenced by the evil that surrounds us. However, evil can never penetrate holiness. That is why Jesus died for our sins—to make us holy and spotless before God.

In work and in life, we must be serious about not being yoked with those who are immoral. We often take or remain in jobs led by people who are not in God's will. We have friends who are not in relationship with God. We then wonder why we are not happy and why areas in our life are dysfunctional. Repent and purge yourself of them!

Lord, help me to always have holy people close to me. I praise You for giving me the gift of these wonderful people.

Do you trust God's wisdom and listen to His words in your heart? He is often telling you to beware of or remove yourself from situations and/or people who try to tempt you out of His will.

Deuteronomy 28:13 "The LORD will make you the head, not the tail, and you will always mount higher and not decline, as long as you obey the commandments of the LORD, your God, which I order you today to observe carefully."

God is consistent with His promises. If you are in His will and following His commandments, you will prosper. If this is true, why doesn't everyone do it? I believe there are two reasons. First, they don't have a true faith. Second, they rely on their own strength, not the Lord's, and are influenced by evil intentions.

God desires to bless us with His gifts in a way far superior to how parents want to bless their children. All we need to do is say "Yes" and follow Him.

Lord, I say "Yes" to You today and always. Bless me, indeed! I praise You for the gift of faith.

How do you say "Yes" to the Lord every day? Do you find your faith growing when you say "Yes"? Do you need to work on saying yes to God every day? He finds ways to give you the opportunities to say "Yes." He may send you a person in need or call you, through yourself or others, to use your God-given talents. He waits for you to respond and say "Yes" to Him!

Galatians 1:8 "But even if we or an angel from heaven should preach [to you] a gospel other than the one that we preached to you, let that one be accursed!"

In our lives, we will hear many "gospels." It might be the gospel of secular humanism or whatever's new or old. In this age, the gospel that pursues sex, money and power is prevalent and runs rampant.

You might think you are above temptation. Think again. The question is whether you will fall prey to it. Monitor your actions and speech to ascertain the level of the world's gospel that has penetrated your life. Then seek the truth. Repent and ask for God's grace to do His will.

Come Lord Jesus, purify our souls so that we may remain faithful to Your calling. I praise You for calling me.

Do you ask God to purify your heart? Do you use the Sacrament of Reconciliation? When you sin, you fall from His grace. Desire His grace once more and repent. Your soul will continue being faithful in the Lord. Rejoice!

Galatians 1:10 "Am I now currying favor with human beings or God? Or am I seeking to please people? If I am still trying to please people, I would not be a slave of Christ."

I believe the question of whom we try to please is one of the most critical for all of us. When speaking of "people," could we be speaking of our spouse or family? They are not excluded from the human beings mentioned in this Scripture passage. I can say I have sinned by putting my family first, at times, before serving God and doing His will. When I put God first, I know I am in God's will.

To be a slave of Christ means nothing is in the way of serving Him. It can't be a job, family, marriage, love of sports or any activity. It must be our pure love for Christ. That is very hard for most of us. Many fall by the wayside because they think it is too difficult. Ask for God's grace to help you put Him first in your life!

Lord, may I answer the question of whom I am trying to please by showing you my desire to please You and put You first always. I praise You for that desire.

Do you succeed in putting God first in your life? No one is perfect. When you fail in loving Him perfectly, seek forgiveness and forgive yourself.

1 Peter 2:17 "Give honor to all, love the community, fear God, honor the king."

You've got to love Peter. He is a straight shooter and very practical. First, he states we should put the other person first by paying them honor. Most people want to do that in reverse. Secondly, he wants us to love each other in the community as Christ loves us.

Thirdly, we should show our fear of God because humility will help us to recognize who we are versus God. Only then will we understand that it is only through God we do anything good. Finally, there is the practical aspect of honoring those in authority—so that we may live in peace. Yes, we are headed to a New Kingdom, but why not live in peace while we're here.

Lord, may I love, honor and respect those I am with today, while fearing You at all times. I praise You for the gift of fear of the Lord.

Do you know when you fear the Lord you are praising Him? Do you know how much joy that brings Him? How joyful are you when your God is happy with you?

Psalm 145:18 "The LORD is near to all those who call upon him...in truth."

Why do you think the Psalmist added the words "in truth?" Doesn't it matter if we just call on Him without regard to truth? The reality is that without truth we cannot be in communion with God. Jesus clearly told us He is the "the way, the truth, and the life."

God is always near us when we call to Him for help and when listening for answers to our prayers. He will help us get through our problems by His strength. If you feel like giving up, shout to Him, and He will answer you and shower you with His grace. Jesus is faithful, and He will always strengthen us in our hour of need.

Lord, I call upon You today to hear the desires of my heart. I praise You for being faithful.

Do you tell God all your desires? He will be faithful and answer you. Will you be open to what He says to you?

Deuteronomy 31:6 "Be brave and steadfast; have no fear or dread of them, for it is the LORD, your God, who marches with you; he will never fail you or forsake you.

Each year is the most exciting year of my life and also the most challenging one. It doesn't always go according to my plan, but it happens the way the Lord wants. And, it is what the Lord wants to teach me. Sometimes my year is filled with peaks and valleys to the point I could scream and, in fact, do scream and ask God why He is allowing things to unfold this way.

Throughout each year, the Lord whispers in my ear, "Do not be afraid. I am with you. Do not fear for you are my beloved, my chosen one, to go forth and spread my gospel, my Good News." God is always with us, and if we have faith, He will act.

Lord, thank You for teaching me to be steadfast and to not fear anything because You will never fail me. I praise You for another blessed year.

Do you feel less anxiety and fear knowing God will never fail You? He is beside you, day in and day out, and ever present!

Joshua 6:10 "But the people had been commanded by Joshua not to shout or make any noise or outcry until he gave the word: only then were they to shout."

Obedience is essential to doing the will of the Lord. Joshua understood this. When the angel of the Lord said, "Remove your sandals," Joshua obeyed. When the Lord gave specific instructions on what to do with Jericho, Joshua did not say, "What about this approach or idea instead?" Once again, he obeyed.

During the siege of Jericho, all the people followed this disciple. When they finally were told to shout, they did, resulting in the capture of the city. This kind of obedience is what Jesus asks of us. God will tell us what to do. We then have the choice of obeying or doing it our way. When we do it our way, the result is always the same. Disaster!

Lord, teach me to be obedient to You at all times and in all things. I praise Your name!

Do you ever find yourself not choosing God's way? When failure is actualized, what then? Do you turn to Him for forgiveness? Do you ask God for His guidance once again?

Genesis 2:24 "That is why a man leaves his father and mother and clings to his wife, and the two of them become one body."

Today is my wedding anniversary. We have been married more than 40 years. Indeed, we are living the pledge, "In good times and in bad, for better or for worse." We have had plenty of both. My wife is the greatest blessing God has given me. She represents everything good about life and the Lord. Her faith, patience, laughter, love and support are only a few of the many things I treasure.

God created marriage so that a man and a woman may be of "one body." That spiritual and physical union equates to the union He desires with us. This is true intimacy and is based upon giving yourself to each other. In marriage, it is also "Jesus over you."

Lord, I thank and praise You for the gift of my wife.

Pray for all marriages. Do you pray for your parents', other family members' and friend's marriages?

Hebrews 11:21 "By faith Jacob, when dying, blessed each of the sons of Joseph and 'bowed in worship, leaning on the top of his staff.'"

We are only a few days before Christmas, a time of hustle and bustle, confusion, stress and, at times, worry. Often, we try to remember why we are making the decisions we make. Is it for Jesus and His kingdom or just to please someone else?

One of the greatest gifts you can give your children is to bless them. God honors a parent blessing their child. Like Jacob, who experienced the fruits of being blessed by his father, you can give your children the eternal grace of blessing them spiritually as well as physically for this world. It is a true gift that costs no money but is more valuable than anything you can ever give them.

Lord, may I bless my children, grandchildren, family and friends this Christmas season as You, my Father, have blessed me. I praise You for this blessing!

You may find it difficult to bless some people because they lack or have so little faith. Will you quietly bless them in your heart when you hug them, speak to them and when they sleep? Blessing the people in your life is a great gift. Do you find the time and your own way to bless them?

December 20

Revelation 22:12 "'Behold, I am coming soon. I bring with me the recompense I will give to each according to his deeds.'"

God is good, merciful and kind. He is also just. He will provide the reward for what we do here on earth or allow punishment in accordance to what we have reaped. It is up to us to determine what we receive when we die. For it is God's will that each human is saved. His desire for us is eternal salvation.

In this period of Advent, it is important that our patience turns into hope for the future on earth, just as it will be in heaven. It is up to us how we live now and in the future. Accept God and live!

Lord, help me to wait for You with patience, love and perseverance. I love and praise You!

Are you preparing yourself for His coming, at all times? In doing this, know that He may not come during your earthly lifetime, but you should be preparing your heart for everlasting life in Him. It is well worth it to act now, as He asks!

December 21

Psalm 91:10 "No evil shall befall you,/ nor shall affliction come near your tent."

How would you like this to be true in your life? Do you believe it is possible? Certainly, when you go to the Lord in faith, He will protect you from all evil. This promise is in the Lord's Prayer, and many references in Scripture guarantee it.

What about affliction and its affinity to our life? Certainly, an affliction of sickness or disease is often hard to understand. However, it is certain Jesus will heal illness when we ask Him, if it is in His will. He does not bring affliction upon us. Affliction is something that is a part of life, but our response to it does not need to be one of grumbling, agony or unhappiness, rather of hope and compassion.

Lord, I praise and thank You for Your protection against all evil and affliction.

Do you ask the Lord for His protection in Jesus' name? This is a very powerful prayer and He will honor any request that is in His perfect will and in the name of Jesus.

Psalm 51:11 "Turn away your face from my sins,/ and blot out all my guilt."

When we sin, if we are of the Lord, we feel awful. We are guilt-ridden because the Holy Spirit is reminding us we have been bought and sold by the blood of the Lamb and we are His. We are disappointed in ourselves for choosing the world and/or our flesh over the love of the Lord.

We don't want the Lord to remember our sins. Guess what? It is true! God doesn't remember them when we truly confess our sins. That means we must sincerely repent and turn away from them. Does that mean we will never sin again? Not likely, but it does mean that we are moving toward holiness.

Lord, I praise Your name for Your love and forgiveness.

Do you have great hope no matter what? God will always forgive Your honest heart and will always love you!

Luke 1:45 "Blessed are you who believed that what was spoken to you by the Lord would be fulfilled."

Here we are, two days before Christmas. It is hard to believe. Where did the year go? Has it been a year since you began this spiritual journey? Do you find you have grown closer to Christ or have you moved further away? Do you find your heart "burning" with the love of Christ? Overall, I have grown tremendously in the Lord. But, I look up and see how far up the mountain I still need to go to be even remotely at the point of the holiness I strive for.

One key barometer for faith is to imitate the holiness of Mary. Without question, she believed when she heard the Word of the Lord speaking to her. If you trust God, then He will act powerfully in your life.

I praise and thank You Lord for giving me the faith to believe Your Word.

Do you meditate on putting God first and foremost in your life? Do you believe in His Word, His truth and His son, Jesus Christ?

December 24

Luke 2:10 "The angel said to them, 'Do not be afraid; for behold, I proclaim to you good news of great joy that will be for all the people.'"

On this Christmas Eve, what is the Good News of great joy in your life? Is life exciting to you? If joy is found in your job, car or anything of this world, then you need to reflect on priorities. The joy in our lives should only come from love and the Lord. We love our families and they bring us great joy. However, the joy is not just the family, but in the love we have in our hearts for them. This same love is for all God's people, and most of all, for the love of Jesus. This love transcends everything else in our life.

It is the source of all joy!

I praise You Lord for being the great joy in our lives.

Is Jesus your reason for living? Are you joyful in His love through all the days of your life? Praise Jesus our Savior, King of all kings! O come let us adore Him!

Luke 2:11 "'For today in the city of David a savior has been born for you who is Messiah and Lord.'"

Praise and glory to God in the most high! Our Savior is born! Someone who will deliver us from bondage and sin. He will lead us into His heavenly kingdom.

I feel strongly this day is one of great joy, not because of gifts or family time, but for the holiness of God humbling Himself and becoming a sacrifice so that we may live forever.

What are your Christmas memories? It is great when those memories are ones of praise and worship and not only material things. This is not easy to do, but it is the foundation for all happiness. As you celebrate this Blessed Day, ask the Lord to take possession of your heart, that you may become pure and holy with your praise and worship.

Lord, I praise You for being the Messiah, Savior and Deliverer.

Jesus always knew His purpose. In His infancy He knew He was on earth to bring us to know God through Him. How does that speak to your heart during this Christmas season?

December 26

Luke 2:20 "Then the shepherds returned, glorifying and praising God for all they had heard and seen, just as it had been told to them."

I don't know about you, but the day after Christmas is usually a day of totally exhaustion. Today I can reflect upon the Christmas season and the many blessings I have received. Unfortunately, it often isn't a season in which I spend enough time focusing and praising God for who He is and what He has done for me.

The shepherds had their Christmas. They received many blessings from the miracle sighting of the angels and the powerful words spoken to them. And then they witnessed Mary, Joseph and the baby Jesus in the manger. What an amazing experience! They continued spreading the Good News and praising and glorifying God for all they had heard and seen. Perhaps we should do the same today.

Lord Jesus, I praise Your for Your glory and for the blessings of being my Messiah and Savior.

Do you get caught up in the Christmas hustle and bustle? Take a moment to reflect on the gift God wants you to share with His people. Jesus, Jesus, Jesus!

Luke 2:25 "Now there was a man in Jerusalem whose name was Simeon. The man was righteous and devout, awaiting the consolation of Israel, and the holy Spirit was upon him."

During Advent, the season before Christmas, we focused on patience, waiting and hope. No one ever did that as well as Simeon. He had waited his whole life to fulfill a promise given to him by the Holy Spirit—a promise that he would not die before seeing the Messiah.

His patience and hope blessed Simeon for he did see his Messiah, Jesus. In the same way, we are blessed when we follow the prompting of the Holy Spirit, in His time. It is easy to get discouraged when things don't occur in our time schedule. Simeon is an excellent example for us to follow. At the end of the year, we might feel depressed as we reflect on a year that didn't meet our expectations. Rejoice! The blessings are around the corner.

I praise and thank You Lord for Your many blessings during the year. I patiently wait for the fulfillment of all Your promises.

Do you know every day you have the opportunity to know Jesus? You are in the same position as Simeon. You have an earthly life and an everlasting life in Christ!

December 28

Proverbs 16:7 "When the LORD is pleased with a man's ways,/ he makes even his enemies be at peace with him."

Often during the holidays, we can experience a substantial amount of stress, often due to unmet expectations. We want things done in a certain way or for people to treat us as we think we should be treated. Guess what? That almost never happens! If we are not careful, depression then can set in. Jesus wants us to put other people first at all times. Their hopes, dreams and desires should come before our agenda. This is difficult to do, but when we are given the grace to accomplish it, God makes those people who are in conflict with us resolve their differences. Then peace will enter our hearts and minds

I praise You Jesus for bringing peace to us and to those people with whom we are in conflict.

Is asking God to step in and take over a difficult situation a great blessing for you? How? It isn't always easy, but in the end, it is right, because it is God's will.

December 29

Psalm 107:41 "Lifted up the needy out of misery/ and made the families numerous like flocks."

Our family enjoys giving gifts to those in need during the holidays. One gratifying activity is the "Secret Santa" my wife often does. We leave gifts for a family at the door and run away before they can see us. Often, the family is in the most difficult of times. It could be financial, physical or spiritual. We found this gift could make a huge difference in their lives. It is the thought that someone loves them so much they would sacrifice their time—it can be daily for four weeks! To our knowledge, we have never been discovered. We leave the season knowing the light of Christ shone through us to our "Secret Santa" families.

Lord Jesus, may I always put the needs of the needy before my own. I praise You for taking care of us.

Do you find little or big ways to help the needy? You can find small ways every day of your life to make His Spirit of Christmas come alive. God wants us to love and care for each other every day.

Romans 15:13 "May the God of hope fill you with all joy and peace in believing, so that you may abound in hope by the power of the holy Spirit."

This verse is very precious to me because I received it from the Lord during the hour of my mother's death— a profoundly holy experience. I felt the presence of the Holy Spirit in a powerful way. It was the end of my mother's mortal life and the beginning of her eternal life.

The close of a year is like a death and rebirth experience. The end of a time period we call a year. The hopes and dreams we sought during the year have been fulfilled, denied or postponed. With the New Year, we can rest in the joy of our faith, knowing that through the power of the Holy Spirit, we will have a blessed New Year.

I praise You, Jesus, for the blessings and grace of this year. I look forward, through hope and the power of your Spirit, to a fantastic New Year.

Do you believe God has such wonderful things in store for you and your family? May you see and recognize all of God's blessings in this new year and in all the days of your life!

December 31

Peter 1:3 "Blessed be the God and Father of our Lord Jesus Christ, who in his great mercy gave us a new birth to a living hope through the resurrection of Jesus Christ from the dead."

The year is at an end. As I reflect on the progress of fulfilling the purpose God has for me, I rejoice over the blessings I have received. Most of all, I praise God for the spiritual growth I have been given through grace. For this year, I received hope to become the person that Christ would have me be. I am far from perfect, but I am striving to be holy.

As I enter into the New Year, I ask the Lord to take over my life, my family, my ministries and my work. My desire is to serve Him, but most of all to love Jesus with all my heart, soul and might, and to love my neighbor as myself.

Lord Jesus, grant the people who read this book be blessed and filled with the Holy Spirit in the coming year. I praise You for the gift of fulfilling the purpose of my life!

You have chosen each day to reflect on Scripture, to find new deep meaning in your faith and to praise God more fully. God bless you and all those you love forever! Praise the Lord now and forever!